Disney Melodies

Other Books by Karl Beaudry

Disney Destinies

Disney Melodies

The Magic of Disney Music

Karl Beaudry

Theme Park Press
www.ThemeParkPress.com

© 2015 KARL BEAUDRY

No part of this publication may be reproduced, distributed, or transmitted in any form or by any means, including photocopying, recording, or other electronic or mechanical methods, without the prior written permission of the publisher, except for brief quotations embodied in critical reviews and certain other noncommercial uses permitted by copyright law.

Although every precaution has been taken to verify the accuracy of the information contained herein, no responsibility is assumed for any errors or omissions, and no liability is assumed for damages that may result from the use of this information.

Theme Park Press is not associated with the Walt Disney Company.

The views expressed in this book are those of the author and do not necessarily reflect the views of Theme Park Press.

Theme Park Press publishes its books in a variety of print and electronic formats. Some content that appears in one format may not appear in another.

Editor: Bob McLain
Layout: Artisanal Text

ISBN 978-1-941500-35-4
Printed in the United States of America

Theme Park Press | www.ThemeParkPress.com
Address queries to bob@themeparkpress.com

To my favorite musician—my wife—who didn't realize the implications of asking me to be her accompanist for a clarinet jury 35 years ago.

Contents

Introduction ix

1. The Great Disney Composers 1
2. Was Walt Disney a Musician? 23
3. Disney's Magical Musical Timing 25
4. Disney's Musical Familiarity, Repetition, and Consistency 31
5. Disney Music's Melodic, Harmonic, and Rhythmic Structure 39
6. The Magic of Musical Consistency 49
7. Disney Music's Magical Quality 57
8. Magical Musical Highlights 61
9. A Word about Disney Sounds and Production . 107
10. Final Refrain 111

Appendix 113
About the Author 121
About the Publisher 123
More Books from Theme Park Press 125

Introduction

There are two hobbies in my life that consume much of my time: Disney and music.

When I was 11 years old, my parents took me to Walt Disney World. The year was 1971 and the month was December. If you are a true Disney fan, you've already realized that this was the first Christmas at Walt Disney World. The crowds were massive and the lines were long, but the frustrations were far outweighed by the magical influence that trip had on me. I can clearly remember standing in line at the Transportation and Ticket Center and being in awe of the Monorail overhead, its sleek shape and quiet motors portraying a futuristic preview of what I would see inside the park. I was smitten by the Disney bug and have been back countless times since that first trip, soaking up all I can about the parks and all things Disney.

Music, on the other hand, has been a talent and interest handed down through the family. My parents made sure that I had piano and instrumental lessons from the time I was very young. Now that I'm an adult, I consider myself to be somewhat of an expert with music. I've been performing, writing, arranging, and conducting all my life. Professional, semi-professional, television, church, local, school—you name it—I've experienced it musically. I am a music theory enthusiast and I love the challenge of hearing music and analyzing it in my head for both rhythm and harmony. My wife and I regularly perform concerts together and find music to be a great escape from the realities of the world.

As a result of this combination of interests, I am not surprisingly obsessed with the music of Disney. The only music I have on my iPhone comes from a 2-CD set of Walt Disney World park and attraction music. My ring tone is a portion of the opening theme from "Illuminations: Reflections of Earth". The first notes I play when sitting at the piano are usually familiar phrases from *Beauty and the Beast* or *Aladdin*. And what about my morning wake-up music? You guessed it—the music heard every morning on Main Street, U.S.A. In addition, I'm probably the world's greatest Sherman Brothers fan. (We will discuss the Sherman Brothers at length in this book.)

But my obsession with Disney music has led me to some intriguing questions I've never been able to answer. What is it about Disney music that has me so glued to it? How do they do it? What kind of acoustical science must they be using to draw people in like the Pied Piper's rats? After all, this is Disney we're talking about. It is simply not possible that the music of Disney would just be carelessly recorded and mixed without some vast marketing philosophy to control its existence. There has to be some sort of unwritten conspiracy behind each composition. There must be some sort of formula that infuses each song with a powerful magnet, giving it the ability to move people in one direction or another, convince them to buy something, or control their moods during the day. After all, Disney marketing created the most recognizable icon in the world with three simple circles (right up there with the Coca Cola scripted letters). A company with that level of branding ability is going to study the effects music has on its customers. We know, of course, that music's effects can be powerful. Consider this paragraph from the muzak.com website:

> The power of music is undeniable. Music creates a connection and sets a mood. It can motivate, attract and engage. It can be a competitive advantage and a reason for customers to come in and come back. Let Muzak help you use the widest selection of fully licensed music solutions to create an environment that will enhance your brand and build your business.

Those of us who know Disney's methods can be confident that they have invested an immense amount of time and effort into studying how they use music and how it will affect their ability to gain and keep customers. So what were their conclusions? How do they use music to "trick" their customers into thinking that Walt Disney World is the Happiest Place on Earth? How do they use music and sounds to wrap me around their corporate finger?

Several years ago I started to seek out answers to those questions. Despite my knowledge of music and its construction, I was still not completely sure of what I would discover. My investigation led me to some fascinating realms of musical and psycho-acoustical theories. Of course, my research also led me to Walt Disney World itself many times. (It's a rough job, but somebody has to do it.) I can still remember my amazement at the construction of the theme music for the SpectroMagic Night Time parade along Main Street. It was at that time I decided to push further and truly hunt for some conclusions to satisfy my own curiosity.

This book is a result of my study. I must admit that I have spent far too long on the entire project, but I also know it is one of those things that will possibly never end. On the other hand, I am excited about what I can share with you right now regarding the ingredients in a Disney song (and many other songs) that keep people listening. The book will be covering music (and sound effects) in Disney theme parks and resorts, along with the famous Disney film and television music that one would expect to be included in a study such as this. (Note that I'll be introducing some rather advanced musical terms; I define these for a lay audience in the appendix.)

There are two very important points to be made clear before embarking on this study, or any study of music as it relates to the tastes and preferences of listeners:

- It is impossible to apply what we will discuss here to all Disney music. Because music is an art, there are no comfortable corners that we can fit every song into. While we can emphasize certain characteristics of the better-known songs, we will always run into an inevitable list of hit songs that do not fit into any of our "theories". That is a good thing! It is the variety in music that makes it so wonderful. When one considers the thousands of songs in the Disney repertoire, there can be no doubt that many of them will represent the square song that does not fit into our round hole.

- Many readers will most certainly get through half of this book and start to wonder if there's anything new under the sun. They will read of the various "hooks" within Disney music that make it popular and ask why these same things could not be said about any music. While it is my firm belief that there are certain exclusive characteristics of Disney music, I am also not naïve enough to believe that Disney musicians have a monopoly on the techniques they use. After all, the use of these familiar techniques for all music is most likely what makes it so comforting to us. There are definitely certain features in most popular songs that make their patterns predictable. That ability to predict provides us an unconscious form of relaxation and security, while at the same time increasing our desire to hear the song again. It is clear that Disney does not hold the exclusive patent on the "hooks" we will discuss, but they just may be the best at using them over and over again in an ever-increasing variety of contexts.

So why should I be the one to write this book? Am I the expert on this topic? Absolutely not! But I was truly amazed to find that after years of searching for material on this subject, I could find nothing. There are many great books on the topic of Disney music, but none covering the wonderful features that make it qualified to be "Disney". I look for the behind-the-scenes magical formulas that make Disney what it is and I am rarely disappointed. Since I am also a musician, I find that my "mouse ears" are often tuned to everything going on at the parks and in the movies. As a result, at the very least, the reader of this study can expect a child-like sincerity and excitement, combined with a lifelong passion for and study of both Disney and music.

PS. Throughout this book, you'll find short comments by Disney fans about the kind of Disney music they enjoy, and why it's meaningful to them. I think it's important not just to study Disney music as a quasi-academic topic, but to give examples of its use "in the wild" and the effect it has on people like you and me.

CHAPTER ONE

The Great Disney Composers

It is appropriate to begin a book on Disney music by studying the musicians themselves. Certainly it would be impossible to mention each person who had his hand in Disney music, but the big names do stand out, for good reason. Like the famous Imagineers responsible for the unique attractions and technical wonders within Disney theme parks, Disney musicians have a knack for what the public wants most. They are able to find a winning formula and stick with it, though the context for their music is often eclectic, from dark rides to musicals, sound effects to sound tracks, background music to feature symphonies.

One need only to spend a short time at a Disney park listening to the Main Street musicians, the Voices of Liberty, or the attraction music to know that quality is top priority for anything heard by the public. At the same time, the fondest memories of the great Disney movies are in the sometimes crazy, often emotional melodies that serve to rouse within us thoughts of our own passions and pastimes. Whatever formula Disney uses, musicians are well aware of it and seem to thrive on making it work over and over again.

The following is an overview of the greatest Disney composers and how they contributed to the most well-known legacy of songs that exists today. Every composer cannot be listed, but I have included those responsible for the most popular cartoon songs, musical numbers, film scores, and television themes.

Note: Many song titles will be repeated since composers often cooperated on a musical score. For example, one composer may have written the words while the other arranged the orchestrations or wrote the melodies.

Adair, Tom

> *The Mickey Mouse Club*
>
> *Paul Bunyan*
>
> *The Rainbow Road to Oz*
>
> *Sleeping Beauty*
>
> *Third Man on the Mountain*

Perhaps demanding a chapter all its own, the story of Tom Adair is a fascinating tale of working at a power company as a clerk while writing song lyrics in his spare time. After being discovered in 1941, Adair soon penned Broadway musicals and television theme songs that earned him well-deserved fame.

Adair teamed up with Disney staff composer Buddy Baker to compose memorable lyrics for many of his famous melodies. However, he is perhaps best-known for his work with television theme songs, including those for *My Three Sons*, *F Troop*, *Hogan's Heroes*, *I Dream of Jeannie*, and *Gomer Pyle*.

Ashman, Howard

> *Aladdin*
>
> *Beauty and the Beast*
>
> *The Little Mermaid*
>
> *Oliver & Company*

It is easy to imagine how much of a household name Howard Ashman would have become were it not for a tragic early death, the result of AIDS when he was only 40 years old. Ashman partnered with Alan Menken to write unforgettable and delightful songs that helped to revive the animated musical genre for

Disney. Who can think of *The Little Mermaid* without humming the tunes to "Under the Sea" and "Kiss the Girl"? In addition, it is said that the songs he wrote for *Beauty and the Beast* rescued a movie that was originally planned to be a non-musical and perhaps headed to the trash heap without his help.

Howard Ashman was the recipient of Grammy, Golden Globe, and Academy awards for his efforts. He became a Disney Legend in 2001 and will long be remembered for his genius for creating lyrics that told stories in realistic, yet joyful ways.

Atencio, Xavier

The Haunted Mansion

Pirates of the Caribbean

Francis Xavier Atencio (or "X" Atencio, as he is more commonly called) was a shy person and never one to push his way onto the scene. He was reluctant to send his sample portfolio to Disney because he didn't think it was as good as what Disney was looking for. If it weren't for an instructor that pushed him, he may never have had the start he needed for what turned out to be a stellar career.

On the day he was hired, he was so excited that he ran all the way home yelling, "I got a job at Disney!" After being transferred to WED (the division responsible for building Disneyland), Walt asked Atencio to write the "script" for the Pirates of the Caribbean attraction. Disney attractions were not just rides. Every portion of Disneyland would need to have a story. Not even the Carrousel would be built without a back story to guide its development! The Pirates attraction would need a back story with scenes and script for proper flow and for entertainment value. Atencio was being asked to write "mini-movies" that would be the content base for each attraction scene.

In a final meeting with Walt for the Pirates attraction, Atencio suggested that there should be a little tune playing during the boat ride. He even had an idea for the melody and some appropriate lyrics. Atencio assumed that Walt would agree and send the task over to the Sherman Brothers to write the song. Imagine his surprise when Walt instead asked him to take the words over to George Bruns to add a melody. (Bruns was a talented Disney composer responsible for the tunes on many of the Disney attractions.) Atencio was now officially a song writer for Walt Disney and the rest is history. One cannot imagine the Pirates of the Caribbean or Haunted Mansion attractions without the clever and catchy songs providing the background music.

X Atencio became a Disney Legend in 1996 and retired in 1984 after working 47 years with the company.

Baker, Buddy

Napoleon and Samantha

The American Adventure (Epcot)

The Fox and the Hound

The Haunted Mansion

Impressions de France (Epcot)

Innoventions (Disneyland)

The Many Adventures of Winnie the Pooh (Walt Disney World)

The Mickey Mouse Club

The Rainbow Road to Oz

Wonders of China (Epcot)

Swamp Fox

Universe of Energy (Epcot)

Buddy Baker got his start with the Disney Company simply because a former student of his (George Bruns) needed help with his work load. Bruns was given assignments for both television and the parks, and, when the work grew overwhelming, he gave the park assignments to Baker. As a result, Baker quickly amassed a long list of orchestrations and scores, and became a very popular composer himself. One special talent of his was orchestration: the process of creating orchestral music out of simple arrangements or tunes that were written by other composers. For example, while the Sherman Brothers wrote the tune for "it's a small world", Baker created the orchestral versions heard within the attraction itself.

Baker became a Disney legend in 1998 and passed away in 2002. His musical talent will long be remembered since it is heard over and over each day at Disney parks around the world.

Blackburn, Tom W.

Davy Crockett and the River Pirates

Davy Crockett, King of the Wild Frontier

Johnny Tremain

Westward Ho the Wagons!

Perhaps Thomas Blackburn's biggest claim to fame is the lyrics to the smash hit, "The Ballad of Davy Crockett". (George Bruns wrote the music.) On December 15, 1954, the television mini-series *Davy Crockett* aired to great acclaim. The theme song sold over ten million copies and spawned a worldwide craze. Along with the song itself, the famed coonskin cap became a huge seller for both children and adults.

Blackburn wrote for other Disney programs, such as *Johnny Tremain*, but received most of his work as a ghost writer for fiction authors. His time with Disney was short-lived, but certainly productive from a financial point of view.

Bruns, George

The Adventures of Bullwhip Griffin

Babes in Toyland

Davy Crockett and the River Pirates

Davy Crockett, King of the Wild Frontier

The Fighting Prince of Donegal

Goliath II

Johnny Tremain

The Mickey Mouse Club

Paul Bunyan

Perri

Pirates of the Caribbean

Robin Hood

The Saga of Andy Burnett

The Saga of Windwagon Smith

Sleeping Beauty

Tonka

Westward Ho the Wagons!

Zorro

When George Bruns was hired by Walt Disney to write the musical score for *Sleeping Beauty*, no one could have imagined the 22-year Disney career that would follow. Bruns received an Academy Award nomination for his work with *Sleeping Beauty*, and the reward he received for writing "The Ballad of Davy Crockett" was nearly worldwide fame and a spot at the top of the Hit Parade for 6 months.

Bruns contributed to over 200 movies, television shows, and attractions during his career with Disney. He is perhaps best known for cooperating with X Atencio in the writing of "Yo Ho (A Pirate's Life for Me)", a song never forgotten by anyone who has enjoyed the Pirates of the Caribbean ride. He also composed the memorable score for Disney's *The Jungle Book*.

He was named a Disney legend in 2001.

Churchill, Frank

The Adventures of Ichabod and Mr. Toad

Bambi

Dumbo

The Flying Mouse

Funny Little Bunnies

The Golden Touch

Peter Pan

The Reluctant Dragon

The Robber Kitten

Santa's Workshop

Snow White and the Seven Dwarfs

The Tortoise and the Hare

The Three Little Pigs

Who Killed Cock Robin?

Part of the magic of Disney music is that it is introduced to the public at the most appropriate times. When Frank Churchill was asked to write a song for *The Three Little Pigs*, his overly simple "Who's Afraid of the Big Bad Wolf?" became a hit because it spoke directly to the "wolf" of financial problems being caused by the Great Depression. America needed an encouraging theme song and Churchill provided the right combination of simplicity and lightheartedness, along with a reminder not to be afraid.

As a result of his initial success, Churchill was asked to score *Snow White and the Seven Dwarfs* and was responsible for such great songs as "Whistle While You Work" and "Some Day My Prince Will Come". Since *Snow White* was such a great success, Churchill became Disney's supervisor of music and went on to contribute many more valuable scores over a 12-year period.

He became a Disney legend in 2001.

Debney, John

Chicken Little

The Emperor's New Groove

Hannah Montana: The Movie

Hocus Pocus

I'll Be Home for Christmas

Inspector Gadget

The Jungle Book

My Favorite Martian

Old Dogs

The Pacifier

The Princess Diaries

The Princess Diaries 2: Royal Engagement

Snow Dogs

White Fang 2: Myth of the White Wolf

It would seem that John Debney was destined to work with the Disney Company. His father was a producer for Disney on such great shows as *Zorro* and *The Mickey Mouse Club*. However, Debney's talents were obviously with music, and when Buddy Baker asked him to arrange music for use in the Disney parks, his long list of musical contributions began to take shape.

Unlike many of the Disney composers, Debney tended to work for a large number of different film studios, but he always was available to lend his talents to Disney films when needed. Perhaps his best-known work is the score for the film *Cutthroat Island*, though his career is so extensive and critically acclaimed, it is likely that we will be hearing much more of his music in the coming years.

Dodd, Jimmie

The Mickey Mouse Club

M-I-C-K-E-Y M-O-U-S-E! Who can forget the famous theme song for the *Mickey Mouse Club*? Jimmie Dodd was a prolific song writer and was credited for at least 400 songs during his lifetime. However, we included only one here because it was so significant. Dodd was the television host of the *Mickey Mouse Club* and won the hearts of Disney fans the world over with his easy-going style and musical expertise. Known as a kind and gentle person, Dodd was the perfect host for a program that became a favorite among children.

Dodd had an extensive musical resume before joining Disney: he studied at several music schools and worked with the USO and several famous musicians. However, it was the call from his friend Disney animator Bill Justice that introduced Dodd to the world of Disney, though the request at the time was only for Dodd to write a simple song to be used as an animation background. As the story goes, Walt heard the song and immediately proclaimed that Dodd should be part of the *Mickey Mouse Club*.

Jimmie Dodd died in 1964 and was named a Disney Legend in 1992.

Fain, Sammy

Alice in Wonderland

Peter Pan

The Rescuers

Sleeping Beauty

Sammy Fain taught himself how to play the piano by ear. During his early years, he made the right connections and began to compose music that soon made him popular among Broadway musicians. Songs like "Let a Smile Be Your Umbrella" and "I'll Be Seeing You" brought him fame and opportunity that eventually led him to Walt Disney.

As a Disney composer, Sammy Fain took part in producing great movie scores such as *Alice in Wonderland*, *Peter Pan*, and *The Rescuers*.

He passed away in 1989 at the age of 87.

Gerrard, Matthew

Brother Bear 2

Camp Rock

The Cheetah Girls 2

Cinderella III: A Twist in Time

Cory in the House

The Fox and the Hound 2

Hannah Montana

Herbie: Fully Loaded

High School Musical

High School Musical 2

High School Musical 3: Senior Year

Ice Princess

The Lizzie McGuire Movie

The Pacifier

The Princess Diaries 2: Royal Engagement

Stuck in the Suburbs

Zenon: Z3

Originally from Canada, Matthew Gerrard got his start very early. He played piano and bass guitar as a young child and even began writing music in his teen years. It didn't take long for people to take notice of his abilities, however, and he was eventually writing music for some very big names. Matthew is perhaps best-known for his smash hit "Breakaway" that was written for Kelly Clarkson. However, when it comes to Disney music, he has truly made a name for himself with a prolific *High School Musical* repertoire.

Gerrard has contributed musically to popular Disney films such as *Hannah Montana, The Pacifier, The Santa Clause 2,* and *Cheaper by the Dozen.* He continues to produce song after song and hit after hit for the ever-popular teen music genre that has propelled Disney ahead in musical circles over recent years. In a recent twist to his career, he was asked to create the theme song for Hong Kong Disneyland, foreshadowing what could possibly be a larger presence of his music at parks and resorts throughout the world.

Gilbert, Ray

The Adventures of Ichabod and Mr. Toad

Make Mine Music

Melody Time

Song of the South

The Three Caballeros

Ray Gilbert won an Oscar for one of the most memorable songs ever written, "Zip-a-Dee-Doo-Dah", for the Disney film, *Song of the South*. Fans of the Donald Duck films will also remember the great lyrics from "The Three Caballeros", which still plays as a theme song (though edited from the original) on the Gran Fiesta Tour in the Mexico Pavilion at Epcot.

Gilbert's lyrics have been performed by some great names, including Bing Crosby, Nat "King" Cole, and Perry Como. Interestingly enough, he started his career as a lyrics translator, something that is much more difficult than it sounds due to rhythmic constraints

Gilbert passed away in Los Angeles at the age of 63.

Gilkyson, Terry

The Aristocats

The Jungle Book

The Moon-Spinners

Run, Cougar, Run

Savage Sam

The Scarecrow of Romney Marsh

Swiss Family Robinson

The Three Lives of Thomasina

Born in 1916, Terry Gilkyson waited until he was over 30 years old before pursuing a musical career. He moved to California specifically to become a folk singer and, along the way, became song writer for the movies and television. He won an Academy Award for his song "The Bare Necessities", the well-known tune from the movie *The Jungle Book*.

When Gilkyson was just 40 years old, he formed a group, the Easy Riders, that would truly be his claim to fame. The group recorded some major hits, including the song "Marianne" which sold over one million copies. His work with Disney came after the Easy Riders disbanded.

Harline, Leigh

The Cookie Carnival

Fun and Fancy Free

Funny Little Bunnies

The Grasshopper and the Ants

The Night Before Christmas

The Old Mill

Peculiar Penguins

Pinocchio

Snow White and the Seven Dwarfs

The Wise Little Hen

Wynken, Blynken, and Nod

Perhaps the one sing that identifies with the Disney Company today more than any other is the beloved "When You Wish Upon a Star". The sophistication of this song and many others from the pen of Leigh Harline puts him in a class by himself as a truly symphonic composer. His songs were more than just a simple melody with added orchestration. They had a fullness all their own that cried out for specific orchestrations.

When Harline joined Disney in 1932, he was asked to write the music for dozens of animated shorts, including many of the Silly Symphonies films and *The Old Mill*, but it was his work (along with that of Frank Churchill) with *Snow White and the Seven Dwarfs* that set him apart. Harline received an Oscar nomination for "Someday My Prince Will Come". He would go on to write some of the greatest Disney songs for the film *Pinocchio*, including the aforementioned "When You Wish Upon a Star".

Since that time, this one song has been used for television shows, television commercials, theme park entertainment, and fireworks spectaculars. It is altogether appropriate for the greatest of Disney songs to speak of dreams and wishes that will one day come true!

Leigh Harline died in 1969 and became a Disney Legend in 2001.

John, Sir Elton

Aida

The Lion King

The Lion King 1 ½

Though Elton John's relationship with Disney was short-lived, his name garnered a lot of attention during the public anticipation of *The Lion King*. An immensely popular singer and songwriter already, Elton John was initially unsure about whether he should be writing for a Disney movie. Nevertheless, he collaborated with Tim Rice (lyrics) to create some of the most memorable songs ever written for an animated Disney film.

The soundtrack for *The Lion King* earned three Academy Award nominations and the soundtrack was a top seller for many years. When *The Lion King* also became a Broadway hit, the awards kept coming, including six Tony Awards and a Grammy. In 1998, Elton John was knighted by the Queen of England, and he was inducted as a Disney legend in 2006.

Leven, Mel

The Adventures of Bullwhip Griffin

Babes in Toyland

It's Tough to Be a Bird

The Litterbug

One Hundred and One Dalmatians

101 Dalmatians II: Patch's London Adventure

Born in Walt Disney's home town of Chicago 13 years following Walt's birth, Mel Leven became an outdoor sportsman with a true talent for writing music. While he did get involved in some unusual recording activities (such as the squeaky voice of Snoopy), he was perhaps best-known for the songs he wrote for the Walt Disney Company. His most famous song was the delightfully evil "Cruella de Vil" from *One Hundred and One Dalmatians*. Leven was also responsible for the lyrics of the *Babes in Toyland* songs (since that film was more of an operetta, it had an unusually large number of songs and not much non-musical dialogue).

While Leven was able to write for such greats as The Andrews Sisters, Nat "King" Cole, and Dean Martin, his most productive years were as a composer with Disney.

He died in 2007 at the age of 93.

Menken, Alan

Aladdin

Beauty and the Beast

Enchanted

Hercules

Home on the Range

The Hunchback of Notre Dame

King David

The Little Mermaid

Newsies

Pocahontas

Who Discovered Roger Rabbit?

With eight Academy Awards for music, Alan Menken has shown himself to be an amazing talent with a knack for writing memorable and inspiring songs that truly bring animated characters to life. It is interesting, however, that Menken first went to college as a pre-med student, later changing his major to music and finding the perfect niche for his talents.

Menken joined the Disney music team in 1987 when he and Howard Ashman teamed together to write the score for *The Little Mermaid*. Other great movie scores followed, such as *Aladdin, Pocahontas, Tangled, Enchanted,* and many others. His songs are rich in emotion and imagination, while carrying a simple melody that lingers on in the mind of all who hear.

Alan Menken was named a Disney legend in 2001 and continues to add to his long list of Disney contributions.

Morey, Larry

The Adventures of Ichabod and Mr. Toad

Bambi

Ferdinand the Bull

The Reluctant Dragon

Snow White and the Seven Dwarfs

So Dear to My Heart

Larry Morey never got the credit he deserved for such a rich history of song writing talent. He joined the Disney Company during the greatest years for animation and wrote songs for animated shorts as well as full-length movies. The fact that he was a "co-writer" for most of the major hits, however, may have contributed to the idea that not a lot of people knew who he was. For the great short animation *Ferdinand the Bull*, for example, he collaborated with composer Albert Hay Malotte. For other great projects, he worked together with the better-known Frank Churchill.

Many do not realize that a film such as *Snow White and the Seven Dwarfs* will often require a great number of songs of which only a few will be chosen for the final cut. For *Snow White*, Morey was involved in writing over two dozen songs, many of which were not chosen to be included in the final product. Fortunately, the songs that were included brought Academy Award nominations which Morey shared with his co-writers.

Morey passed away at the young age of 66 in California.

Nevil, Robbie

Brother Bear 2

Camp Rock

The Cheetah Girls 2

Cory in the House

Hannah Montana

High School Musical

High School Musical 2

High School Musical 3: Senior Year

The Pacifier

Stuck in the Suburbs

Robbie Nevil was a born musician. He played guitar as a child and signed his first publishing deal at the age of 25. His musical career following that point was a blur of solid hits and hot-selling albums.

When Nevil collaborated on an unrelated album project with Matthew Gerrard in 2006, he was naturally asked to continue working with Gerrard on his ongoing Disney projects. As a result, Nevil became involved with some of the hottest Disney music of the time, including *The Cheetah Girls, High School Musical,* and *Hannah Montana*. It is likely that we will be seeing much more work from Nevil in the near future.

Newman, Randy

A Bug's Life

Cars

James and the Giant Peach

Monsters, Inc.

The Princess and the Frog

Toy Story

Toy Story 2

Some of the greatest films ever made by Disney were in cooperation with Pixar. There are few Disney fans that have not appreciated the partnership that created films such as *Toy Story, A Bug's Life, Toy Story 2, Monsters, Inc.,* and *Cars*. Fortunately, the composer chosen for these films was Randy Newman, who was nominated 20 times for Oscars in various musical categories.

Perhaps the greatest project ever penned by Newman was the Disney movie *The Princess and the Frog*. Newman's familiarity with the culture and history of his home town of New Orleans likely contributed to the joyful, poignant, and moving music of the film. While the story itself was top-notch, many film viewers are quick to note that the music was a fabulous representation of New Orleans and its diverse musical culture.

Randy Newman was inducted as a Disney Legend in 2007.

Rice, Sir Tim

Aida

Aladdin

Beauty and the Beast

King David

The Lion King

The Lion King 1 ½

There is so much that could be said about Sir Timothy Miles Bindon Rice. He is best-known for his relationship with Andrew Lloyd Webber and the phenomenal musical productions they produced together, including *Joseph and the Amazing Technicolor Dreamcoat, Jesus Christ Superstar,* and *Evita.*

As a writer for Disney, Tim Rice collaborated with Alan Menken and Elton John to compose Academy and Grammy Award-winning songs, including "A Whole New World" from *Aladdin*.

Rice's brilliance with lyrics resulted in a star on the Hollywood Walk of Fame and an induction into the Songwriter's Hall of Fame. He was inducted as a Disney legend in 2002 and continues to be remembered as the writer who helped Disney regain the lead as a quality producer of animated films.

Sherman, Richard M. and Robert B.

The Absent-Minded Professor

The Adventures of Bullwhip Griffin

The Aristocats

Bedknobs and Broomsticks

Big Red

Bon Voyage!

Carousel of Progress

The Enchanted Tiki Room

Follow Me, Boys!

The Gnome-Mobile

The Happiest Millionaire

The Horsemasters

In Search of the Castaways

It's a Small World

Johnny Shiloh

The Jungle Book

The Legend of Lobo

Mary Poppins

Meet the World

The Miracle of the White Stallions

The Misadventures of Merlin Jones

Monkeys, Go Home!

The Monkey's Uncle

The Moon Pilot

The One and Only, Genuine, Original Family Band

The Parent Trap

Summer Magic

The Sword in the Stone

That Darn Cat!

Those Calloways

The Tigger Movie

Walt Disney's Wonderful World of Color

Winnie the Pooh and the Blustery Day

Winnie the Pooh and the Honey Tree

Winnie the Pooh: Seasons for Giving

As any Disney fan can testify, the Sherman Brothers certainly deserve an entire book dedicated simply to the amazing musical genius that constantly flowed from their pens. An "overview" segment such as this one can in no way do justice to the profound contribution that the Sherman Brothers made not just to Disney but to the world of music itself. Indeed, the English dictionary includes words that were invented by this team and have long since become household terms.

The brothers got their start writing hit songs for well-known singers like Gene Autry. Their first connection to Disney came when they wrote songs for one of the original (and most popular) Mouseketeers, Annette Funicello. It was the long list of hits for Annette that most likely caught the attention of Walt Disney, who hired them as staff composers in 1960.

Numerous stories are told about the tensions that often arose between the two brothers, and the chaotic musical racket that could be heard down the hall from their office at the Disney studio. They would construct a song by playing it over and over, adding a lyric or a different chord each time until they got it right.

The Sherman Brothers will forever be known as the most prolific and beloved musical team ever employed by Disney. They were both inducted as Disney legends in 1990.

Wallace, Oliver

Alice in Wonderland

Darby O'Gill and the Little People

Der Fuehrer's Face

Dumbo

Fun and Fancy Free

The New Spirit

Old Yeller

Peter Pan

In the early years of the 19th century, the popular way to present a film was to have it accompanied by an organist. The great organists would watch the film closely and match their playing style with the mood of the film. Oliver Wallace was considered one of the first and one of the best organists to accompany films.

This talent, of course, is closely related to the matching of background music to animation, something that Wallace was quite comfortable with during his years with Disney. His list of credits is quite long and the quality of his music was enough to garner Academy Awards and flattering comments from the musical greats of his day. Frank Thomas, one of the "Nine Old Men" of Disney animation, called Oliver Wallace a genius.

Wallace died in 1963 at the age of 79. He was inducted as a Disney Legend in 2008.

Wolcott, Charles

The Adventures of Ichabod and Mr. Toad

Make Mine Music

The Reluctant Dragon

Saludos Amigos

Song of the South

The Three Caballeros

Born in Flint, Michigan, Charles Wolcott lived a life that was definitely not cut from a Midwestern mold. He was an excellent pianist and arranger who worked for some of the greatest big band leaders of the era, including Tommy and Jimmy Dorsey, Benny Goodman, and Paul Whiteman. When he joined the Disney Company, he spent his time writing or arranging fabulous film scores.

What was a bit unusual about Wolcott, however, was that he was a member of the Universal House of Justice, a governing body of the Baha'i Faith.

Wolcott passed away in 1987 after being credited as the person who would bring rock-and-roll to motion pictures while working with MGM.

CHAPTER TWO

Was Walt Disney a Musician?

Most of the numerous Disney biographies written over the years meticulously recount the days of Walt's youth in Marceline, Missouri, and his struggles with a domineering father, a difficult paper route, and an indifferent attitude toward school. Walt's early desire to be a cartoonist and his enjoyment of drawing for friends and neighbors are commonly referenced as the true beginnings of his artistic career.

During Walt's childhood, he befriended a fellow student by the name of Walt Pfeiffer, whose family was heavily involved in the theater, vaudeville, and local entertainment. While nothing has been mentioned regarding any musical abilities attributed to Walt himself, we do know that he was often surrounded by musicians (such as the Pfeiffers) and found himself cooperating with them to enhance his own performances.

Since no record of actual musical learning can be found, one could quickly come to the conclusion that Walt was not a musician. On the other hand, there are numerous examples of actions and attitudes in Walt's life that point to an intimate knowledge of music's power and its ability to enhance story telling in any format. Indeed, we find that later in Walt's life he shows a great desire to study and analyze great works of musical genius and a need to meet with music's great composers and conductors of the day. One need only point to the film *Fantasia* to see evidence of a keen sense of musical construction and analysis in Walt's mind. At the same time, his friendship with musical greats, such as Leopold Stokowski, showed that he was "tuned in" to great music and had a knack for using it properly to tell his stories.

So was Walt a musician? Interestingly enough, most dictionaries describe a "musician" as someone who makes music a profession. In this sense, Walt was certainly among the greatest of musicians. While he could not play a violin solo, he could determine whether the solo was appropriate for a particular mood or purpose. Indeed, Walt had the ability to choose particular instruments or styles that would have an almost magical effect on ideas being conveyed through animation.

Disney music just puts me in a good mood! I am a school principal and have a teacher that plays Disney theme park music in his class periodically. When I walk by his room I love matching the music with the ride or park. I think The Lion King and Beauty and the Beast have the best music of any Disney movie. Unfortunately, for those around me, I will sing them for days after hearing them. For some reason, I have an infatuation with the New Age sounds at Epcot around Spaceship Earth and the Land Pavilion.
BK / Texas

CHAPTER THREE

Disney's Magical Musical Timing

When I refer to "timing" in this book, I'm referring to an actual point in time in which a song or sound is produced and made available to the public. (As a musician, I am commonly frustrated by people who confuse their terms and wrongly call the "rhythm" of a song the "timing".) Walt Disney was a timing genius. Over the years, Disney-commissioned musical compositions have gained a reputation for appearing at just the right time for peak popularity.

Perhaps the most obvious example of this involved a song written for a Disney cartoon in 1933 by Frank Churchill. America was suffering through the Great Depression and certainly anything that would help to bring encouragement to households was primed for success. In this case, the song was far from complicated and, in fact, could be analyzed today as something too simple to succeed. The cartoon was *The Three Little Pigs* and the song is still being sung today. "Who's Afraid of the Big Bad Wolf?" was a blockbuster tune that became known and loved the world over.

A purely musical analysis of this song would be harsh and critical, claiming that the words, which consisted of just the words of the title, along with "la la la la la", were those of an amateur or a 3rd grader. The chord structure of the song was similar to that of a nursery rhyme in that it only used the tonic and the dominant chords (for definitions, see the Appendix), something that any beginning guitarist could strum. The rhythmic structure was also as simple as could be, perhaps mimicking the tapping of fingers on a table. From a critical composition viewpoint, perhaps the only saving grace was that the song had a "sequential" melody. (Don't worry, we'll discuss what this is later.) From most angles, though, the song should have gone nowhere.

But the lesson here is that timing is everything! The "big bad wolf" of the Depression was a part of everyone's life. A simple song that could chase away the wolf and cause someone to sing "la la la la la" had every ingredient of a hit song for the day. Its simplicity was its secret formula, and its timing could not have been better. There is speculation that Walt Disney may have timed the release of the cartoon to overcome the mood of the country at the time. On the other hand, the release date could have been the common result of Disney's golden touch. Strategy or not, it seemed that most things Disney released would have enormous success, though not always immediately.

The fact that Walt Disney himself did not write this song may have some readers scratching their heads and wondering, "Why give all the credit to Walt?" Indeed, throughout this book, credit will be given to Walt Disney when numerous composers and sound technicians were certainly on the front line doing all the hard work. However, anyone who has any knowledge of Walt Disney as a leader, or has read any of his numerous biographies, will be quick to note that nothing was presented to the public without Walt's input, editing, adjustment, and overall heavy-handed involvement. With only a few exceptions during the Disneyland planning phase, musician or not, Walt knew what he wanted and absolutely nobody could get away with producing something without him. After Walt's death, the specter of producing something that Walt would not have approved hung over everyone's head for a long period of time. "What would Walt have done?" became the foundation upon which many things were built.

Speaking of Disney songs and timing, is it any coincidence that another song appearing toward the end of the Depression also became a hit, perhaps because of its relationship to overcoming difficulties and following your dream? "When You Wish Upon a Star" won the Academy Award for Best Original Song in 1940 and ranks seventh on the American Film Institute's 100 Greatest Songs list. It is difficult to find anyone not comforted by that wise old grasshopper Jiminy Cricket. The song offers a fascinating study in contrasts, however, because of its intricate chord structure and its difficult-to-sing melody, especially when compared to "Who's Afraid of the Big Bad Wolf?" This significant difference suggests that timing had much to do with the popularity of these songs. For those of us who dream of standing on Main Street, U.S.A. and waiting for that first little white sparkle of "Wishes", the tune of "When You Wish Upon a Star" is something that will never grow tiresome.

Nearly everyone can think of a particular song or sound that marks a significant time in their lives. Dating couples will often adopt "their song" simply because it reminds them of a particular event or occasion during which it was played. Corporations or large organizations will sometimes adopt a theme song for the same reason. The songs often become a rallying cry to assist in overcoming a difficult situation.

Of course, if composers could always predict the perfect timing for a song's publication, there would be far more millionaire composers out there. It is safe to say that while timing is important, hitting that perfect time is often a lucky coincidence. It just seems that where Walt Disney was concerned, a lot of "lucky coincidences" would occur. Of course, this was true of parks and resorts as well as movies and songs, too. Could there be more than just timing that made this possible? We'll discuss that a bit later.

Many would say that luck was not involved at all. They would say that Disney simply monitored the cultural context of the day and then had his composers write songs that would fit in. There is no doubt that this is at least partially true. However, there was no way to predict the popularity of such songs, cultural context or not. How is it that the songs being produced within the walls of the Disney studio seemed to have vaulted to the top despite the myriad other songs being written at the same time? This is where we must assume that there was at least a keen awareness of key cultural attitudes among Disney composers and certainly with Walt himself.

Even though Walt was no longer alive at the time, it is worth considering the year 1995. President Clinton declared November to be National American Indian Heritage Month as our consciousness was focused, at least for a short time, on the contributions and the suffering of the American Indian. Was it simply a coincidence that the song "Colors of the Wind" (from the Disney film *Pocahontas*) won the Academy Award for best song and was one of the highest ranked songs on the radio charts of the day? The timing of the song could not have been better, as people were focused on the plight of the American Indian. Once again, the Disney studio could have taken advantage of current events, but it is more likely that they simply had the same heartbeat as the society around them.

With everything that Walt did, he seemed to have his ear to the ground. He knew what people were thinking. He knew their struggles, their sense of humor, their likes and dislikes. How else can anyone explain his amazing successes with projects that were doomed to failure by the "experts" of the day? Producing a full-length, animated feature, for example, *Snow White and the Seven Dwarfs*, was considered economic suicide. Instead, it made so much money that it kept the Disney studio in business (and let Walt build an even bigger one). How did Walt know this? How did he know that society was ready for such a thing?

There will never be a definitive answer that doesn't touch on the genius of Disney himself. On the other hand, it is difficult to argue that some people just seem to have that sense of success, the golden touch that leads to the perfect ending. It is true, of course, that Walt's life was not all success. On the contrary, Walt suffered huge losses that likely would have discouraged anyone else to the point of quitting. It is the final product, however, that we observe now, and no one can deny the positive result of Walt's persistence, talent, and uncanny timing. Neal Gabler, in *Walt Disney: The Triumph of the American Imagination*, wrote:

> But if one source of Disney's magic was his ability to mediate between past and future, tradition and iconoclasm, the rural and the urban, the individual and the community, even between conservatism and liberalism, the most powerful source of his appeal as well as his greatest legacy may be that Walt Disney, more than any other American artist, defined the terms of wish fulfillment and demonstrated on a grand scale to his fellow Americans, and ultimately to the entire world, how one could be empowered by fantasy how one could learn, in effect, to live within one's own illusions and even to transform the world into these illusions. "When You Wish Upon a Star", the song Disney borrowed from *Pinocchio* for his television theme, was his anthem and guiding principle. The key to his success was, as the journalist Adela Rogers St. John put it, that he "makes dreams come true", or at least gave the impression he did, and that he had "remolded a world not only nearer to his heart's desire, but to yours and mine". In numerous ways, Disney struck what may be the very fundament of entertainment: the promise of a perfect world that conforms to our wishes.

While there are some critics of Walt Disney who will say that he has "cheapened" the arts by "dumbing down" the plots as well as the music, I have a far different opinion. There is a time and place for a Mahler symphony as much as there is for the theme from the *Mickey Mouse Club*. Disney was a genius at finding the right niche for his artistic endeavors and providing an outlet for those seeking a small respite from reality.

Disney music plays a major part in our family's life, from just hearing a song on the radio and bringing a smile to your face reminding you of that special Disney memory, to our daughter with three Disney piano/guitar books that are played in our home on a daily basis. It is amazing how powerful music is, and for a Disney fanatical family like ours, that one song can launch us into a long family discussion of, "Remember when...". And it's funny how our children do not even know some of the biggest names in music but instead call Phil Collins "The Tarzan Guy" and Elton John "The Lion King Guy". We even provide our own soundtrack of WISHES in our car when watching 4th of July fireworks in our hometown in Illinois. Just thinking about Disney music makes me happy."

JF / Illinois

CHAPTER FOUR

Disney's Musical Familiarity, Repetition, and Consistency

Familiarity

We've all heard the term "comfort food" and we know what it means. In times of stress, there is nothing like a hot plate of mac-n-cheese or chicken soup. We all can make up a list without too much effort. The food of our childhood rings us great comfort during the hard times. Why? Our human nature causes us to look to memories of the good times for that "warm and fuzzy" feeling we cannot get enough of.

Besides tastes and aromas, sounds and music are also a large part of those comforting memories. As was mentioned in the last chapter, the song that a couple claims as "their own" and the march that becomes a company's rallying cry are all part of that human desire to use the music of the past as comfort, inspiration, and encouragement for the present.

For many, the sights and sounds of Disney parks and resorts, or the familiar frames of a Disney movie, provide the same comfort as the foods and events of the past. A common testimony of today's adults who were taken to Disneyland or Walt Disney World as a child is that their return visits are like a return to their childhood, and for that reason these places truly represent an escape from the problems of the day.

I can still clearly remember looking upward at hundreds of mechanical birds singing, "In the Tiki Tiki Tiki Tiki Tiki room ...". As an eleven year old, I was in awe of just about everything I saw at Walt Disney World that Christmas season of 1971, just after the Magic Kingdom opened. I can still remember hearing the sounds of Main Street, U.S.A. and the ethereal background music coming from in-ground speakers in Tomorrowland. I can remember that it was nearly impossible to go anywhere on Disney property without some sort of music playing. That was a good thing!

Today, when I head back to the parks, which is often, I am instantly transported to my childhood days with the first strains of music that I hear. I can go to malls or elevators, or be placed on eternal hold to hear some telephone background music, but nothing that I hear in those situations has the same effect as what I hear at Walt Disney World. Why is that? For me, WDW music is "comfort food" for my ears. Stress melts away and the fantasies of childhood become real once again. The feeling is similar to that of listening to Christmas carols beside the tree. These are great moments to be savored.

The songs and sounds of Disney parks and resorts are a result of meticulous planning and study. It is no mistake that my return to Walt Disney World every time would give me the privilege of hearing the same music. While some would insist that the songs be upgraded or completely changed, the Disney Imagineers and musicians know exactly what they are doing. As a returning visitor I need to hear the melodies of *The Music Man*, for example, on Main Street, U.S.A., or I go home disappointed. It is quite possible, in fact, that the effect would be subliminal. If those songs were not playing, would I be disappointed with my day and not even know why?

Repetition

Sometimes the memories being referred to here are caused by a single major event that is etched on someone's mind because of its magnitude. A death in the family, for example, or a tragedy of any sort can embed itself (along with the music or sounds that went with the event) in your mind. On the other hand, memories can be developed as a result of repetition. After all, the best musicians will agree that playing a piece again and again is the key to learning it. Practice *does* make perfect!

Disney songs are often popular because they've been repeated in our ears to the point of saturation. It's as if our brain reserves a special place in the corner for this song because "it ain't going anywhere soon". Along with that "special place" in our brain comes a special connection to the context of the song. For example, riding a particular attraction at Disney World could be a favorite memory. As a result, the theme song for that attraction, especially since it is repeated over and over, becomes the trigger for those wonderful memories. Instantly, the song becomes a favorite song because your brain is telling you that it is.

As an example, the song for "it's a small world" has been the brunt of jokes for decades. (At first, Walt's idea was to have all of the children singing their own national anthems at the same time. Imagine the noise that would have resulted!) On the other hand, the fact that everyone talks about it is proof enough that Disney (with the Sherman Brothers) had a great thing going. Perhaps it is a good strategy to repeat something so often that it becomes ingrained in the mind? A large percentage of the attractions at Disney parks use music that repeats countless times. Consider the Pirates of the Caribbean attraction with the incessant "Yo ho, Yo ho" convincing innocent children everywhere to become pirates. Consider the "Grim, Grinning Ghosts" theme song for the Haunted Mansion and the "Great Big, Beautiful Tomorrow" chorus from the Carousel of Progress. These are all songs we know and love. Would we have had the same opinion had we only heard the songs just once?

There are no doubt some of you that are highly suspect of the entire train of thought here. After all, these attraction songs are repeated simply because they need to last as long as the ride itself, right? There's no strategy in the repetition. My answer to that is, why not? Disney could have easily used a different song for each scene in any of these attractions. Our premise is that using different songs for the same attraction would have been a big mistake and we would not be discussing this at all. The constant barrage of the same melody and lyrics has a definite effect on how we remember the attraction. It is quite possible that the Country Bear Jamboree would be a bit more popular today if the producers of the show considered coming back to a single theme song between each scene as a reprise. My guess is that the song would itself become a subliminal draw to the attraction over the years. Instead, the novelty of the Audio-Animatronics has worn off and there are no longer any lines to this attraction as a result.

Repetition itself can be an art form. Consider that not just words or melody are repeated often, but chords and rhythm as well, and not always at the same time. For example, the unique modal chords of the "Grim Grinning Ghosts" theme from the Haunted Mansion attraction are used as a spooky background theme at the front entrance to Walt Disney World during their ever popular Not So Scary Halloween Party. These chords without the lively rhythms of the attraction sound track are quite effective in setting a scary, solemn mood.

There are, of course, numerous examples of repetition in the orchestral arrangements heard at the various entertainment venues on Disney property. Rarely is a stage show produced that does not have some sort of Disney music medley, complete with dozens of one-phrase references to the great songs. There are even complete shows dedicated to nothing but a review of the great songs and movies. The best example of this is with the *Fantasmic!* night-time show at Disney's Hollywood Studios or Disneyland. Blending a large number of Disney songs together into one large orchestral suite has become a well-known talent and habit for Disney arrangers.

So what is the point here? Isn't Disney just using these hits over and over again because they are popular? Perhaps they don't have enough material and need to re-use what they have?

On the other hand, perhaps they are popular because they are used over and over again? As a regular visitor to Disney resorts, I must admit that some songs I never cared for have grown on me to the point that I excitedly anticipate their performance. My favorite Disney songs are from *Beauty and the Beast*, maybe because my daughter had the movie playing day and night for the entire first year after it was released for home video.

Consistency

Finally, as any business owner will tell you, consistency is an ultra-important factor in assuring high sales of any product. Customers need to know that the product they purchase will perform in the very same way that it did when they first tried it. It is no secret that Disney song writers have a "formula" and they've stuck to it from the start. The proof of this is that there are so many times when we hear a song and instantly say, "Hey, that sounds like Disney music!"

There is an amazing consistency in Disney music, both with lyrics and with music. There seems to be an attitude within the music that screams "Disney" and many cannot put their finger on it. In the preface of *The Disney Song Encyclopedia,* authors Thomas S. Hischak and Mark A. Robinson put it this way:

> But a Disney song is also a state of mind, a lyrical and musical expression of an idea that harkens back to the simple but potent premise that first distinguished Walt Disney more than nine decades ago. Whether it is an animated fairy tale, a live-action adventure, a silly sitcom, or a Disneyland attraction, a Disney production is distinguished by its fine craftsmanship, ambitious goals, and generally optimistic view of life. The same can be said for most of the songs created for these productions. The variety of songs is impressive, from sunny kids' songs and heartfelt blues numbers to rustic folk songs and pulsating rock numbers. Yet there is something positive in the outlook of all these songs. The Disney experience is basically a hopeful one. The productions affirm life and avoid cynicism and despair.

Even when the Disney artists tackle disturbing issues, such as racial inequality or the destruction of the environment, the tone is one of hope. A Disney song, regardless of the many and diverse forms it may take, is a small musical affirmation of what makes life worth living.

The consistency found in Disney songs, however, is much more than an overriding philosophy or mood. A high percentage of Disney songs fit into a pattern that one would expect from a single composer. However, while a few composers were responsible for a large number of Disney songs, the repertoire is by no means limited to those composers only.

Ralph Waldo Emerson said, "Genius borrows nobly." While he was not referring necessarily to music, the same could be said of "genius" composers. Most believe that nothing in music is truly original, but instead every composer draws from his own experiences and tastes that come from listening to other music. If this is true, we could easily come up with a theory as to how much of Disney music has the same feel or sound. To be hired as a Disney musician is to be initiated into a great hall of fame. Certainly a new Disney composer must feel a little like the rookie baseball player who took over Joe DiMaggio's locker. The natural inclination, it seems, would be for the new Disney composer to listen to as much Disney music as possible and then stick to a formula that works. When Walt was alive, he had a tremendous influence on what became "Disney" music and what did not. Interestingly, however, today's Disney music (with few exceptions) has the same "feel" as Disney music of the years gone by. Is that by chance or design?

Just what is the "feel" that we are referring to? While it is impossible to sum up all of Disney music with one simple description, it is perhaps permissible to suggest some possible characteristics. A certain type of orchestration comes to mind. The large orchestration uses the brass (trumpets, trombones, tubas) to enhance melodic passages similar to the pit orchestra in a Broadway show. The strings will often be used for "fluff" parts and flourishes until at the end of a stereotypical Disney song they provide the actual melody at the upper octaves of their range. The horns (including French horn, saxophone, baritone horn) provide a counter melody to fill in at the junction of phrases. The chord structure is often similar to that of a pop ballad, with a familiar ballad rhythm as well, though not as pronounced as it would be if played by a standard rock band instrumentation. Finally, many times there are vocalists providing background choral assistance, sometimes with the effect of a large number of singers, such as an entire choir.

But there is so much more! How does one truly describe the essence of a Disney song? One could argue that "you just know when you are listening to one". On the other hand, the "hooks" discussed in this book could actually be the main ingredients we are seeking. For now, let's move on to another hook and save the "Consistency" topic for later.

CHAPTER FIVE

Disney Music's Melodic, Harmonic, and Rhythmic Structure

On a typical hot and muggy night in July several years back, I sat on the curb of Main Street, U.S.A. in anticipation of my first viewing of SpectroMagic the night-time parade. The spoken intro boomed through the speakers:

> Welcome to the Splendor, the spectacle, the sparkling sensation, where the romance, the comedy and thrill of Disney Fantasies come to electric life. And now the Magic Kingdom proudly presents in a million points of musical light, the Magical World of Disney in SPECTROMAGIC!

It wasn't long after this introduction that I became lost in a musical arrangement that was truly wonderful. Sure, the floats were great, and the technology always amazed me, but this time I caught myself analyzing an ingenious blend of melody, harmony, and especially rhythm. Having studied orchestration and arranging, I began to wonder if anyone really appreciated what I was hearing as much as I did. What I was listening to became an important motivation for what I am writing today. (We'll discuss the music of the parade a bit later.)

While it is true that all songs have some sort of melodic, harmonic, and rhythmic structure, Disney songs use special versions of these features to move themselves to a higher level of attraction for the average music lover. Recall, however, that this is not always the case for all Disney music. "Who's Afraid of the Big, Bad Wolf?" was our example of a song so simple that it barely contained any convincing examples of harmonic or rhythmic structure. On the other hand, the melodic structure of this song might reveal a hook that we have not yet considered.

Sequencing

Most Disney songs take advantage of a simple, yet effective melodic technique known as "sequencing". While there are several interpretations of what a sequence truly is, for our purposes it is the repeating of a short melodic or rhythmic phrase with just enough variation to enhance the overall result. The psychological theory behind the effect is that essentially our minds seek familiarity, even with the sound of something we've just heard. Therefore, when a phrase is repeated, but altered just a bit the second time, excitement and interest is added. The effect is similar to that of suspense or surprise, but it happens so quickly that it is interpreted in our minds as just an extra "plus" for the song.

Of course, this technique is as old as music itself, and Disney's use of it is nothing new. However, a carefully balanced use of this technique with pleasant rhythms and the right orchestration are truly a major reason why Disney songs are Disney songs.

One great example of this technique is with the melody for *Beauty and the Beast*, by Alan Menken. In the illustration below, anyone can pick up the sequencing technique simply by looking, even if they know nothing about music. The notes here are those that are song with the following words:

> Tale as old as time
> True as it can be
> Barely even friends
> Then somebody bends
> Unexpectedly.

The pattern that is set up is repeated. But, as noted by the red arrows in the graphic, the second sequence is altered just a bit. Also, in the second line of music, another sequence occurs, this time with rhythm, but with the melody changing direction.

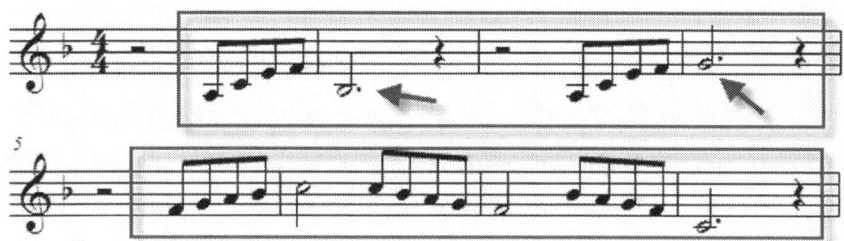

One could also point out that the entire clip being shown could be a single sequence due to the similarities in rhythm. The beauty of this example (no pun intended) is that a good song uses sequencing and a great song can actually have sequencing within sequencing. Many astute musicians have concluded that, with today's music anyway, the more sequencing that occurs, the more likely the song will be a winner.

Here's another example. This one is "A Whole New World" from the animated musical *Aladdin*. For those who cannot read music, suffice it to say that these notes represent the melody that Aladdin sings to Jasmine:

I can show you the world...

In this example, there are three sections making up the sequencing. Two of these sections use the very same notes to start with and then end with different notes. The third section uses the same rhythm but different notes altogether.

It is worth noting here that in both of these examples the chord structure (the non-melody notes that provide the harmony for the song) supporting the melody follows a similar sequencing pattern. In both clips, the chords are the same where the notes are the same, and different where the notes change.

The popularity of these songs is undeniable. Of course, there are a lot more requirements in making a hit song than just sequencing. The point is that sequencing is a great technique for helping to "hook" the listener, and we know that it works.

Remember the first example, "Who's Afraid of the Big, Bad Wolf?" The illustration below probably did not require the red boxes for a visual aid as the sequencing is quite obvious. Perhaps the sequencing helped to make the song a bit more enjoyable? (The notes in the red boxes are the notes for the words "Big, Bad Wolf.")

A fun game to play some time is to think of all the Disney songs you know and pick out the sequences. What is truly interesting is that it is quite possible to find a few without obvious sequences. Ask yourself, "Do I like that song as much as the others?"

Harmonic Structure

What about harmony? For those of you who are not versed in music theory, the harmony in a song is not just two people singing different notes at the same time. While this can be considered harmony, the actual definition is far more complicated. In essence, the entire chord structure and key of a song make up its harmony. Of course, an in-depth study of harmonics and chord analysis is beyond the scope of this book. However, there is much that can be said regarding the common harmonic patterns found in Disney music, while once again emphasizing that not every song has these characteristics.

Much of what is considered "normal" music in today's American culture relies on a series of interchanges between chords to provide a "tension" and "release" that is necessary in quality music. Though difficult to explain in one easy lesson, all songs are based on a specific key and a set of chords that belong to that key. While the keys can change at any point in a song, the normal flow between the chords within the current key is something that we take for granted. For example, if someone were to hum a phrase from a song, just about anyone else who didn't know the song could still most likely guess the final note because their mind has already calculated the appropriate pitch called the "tonic". We all tend to formulate certain progressions from one chord to another in our minds without even realizing it.

One of the best examples of this is the "amen" sung at the end of a hymn or church choral number. A song ends, and then the choir begins to sing a two-note phrase to provide the "amen". Without knowing the song, we can all easily complete that musical phrase in our minds before it happens. Nearly all music contains these little progressions that provide the harmonic interest necessary for a quality piece. When the harmony progresses as we expect it to, it provides comfort and relaxation. When the harmony goes against what we are expecting, there is tension. Any great song should have a little of both, but the point here is that Disney music (more often than not) is harmonically predictable, thus providing the escape and relaxation that it is so famous for.

Like the comfort food we referred to earlier, familiarity is the key to Disney music and a return to the same features in each song provides an instant recognition that causes people to say, "That's a Disney song!" As we are learning, however, those features can be hidden, or at least not quite so obvious. When it comes to harmony, there are techniques used over and over again, perhaps to a fault, that assure us a song is truly Disney. Here is a brief overview of just a few:

- Male/Female duet with a melody line that is harmonized in thirds (two notes that are separated by the interval of a third). Example: Aladdin and Jasmine singing "A Whole New World" or Simba and Nala singing "Can You Feel the Love Tonight?" Of course, the examples of this technique are plentiful among the princess/prince relationships of the early full-length animations such as *Cinderella* and *Snow White*.

- A generous use of secondary dominants. This is a simple harmonic technique to fool the listener into thinking they are in a different key, if only for a very short time. This technique is most often used in the "oompah" or march-like songs. Example: The phrase, "and tomorrow is just a dream away" in the theme song for the *Carousel of Progress* "Great, Big, Beautiful Tomorrow". Another example is in the theme song for the *Pirates of the Caribbean* attraction. The phrase, "Drink up me hearties yo ho!" uses a secondary dominant for just these two measures in each verse. There are countless famous Disney songs that take advantage of this technique. Most of them are the march-like songs such as "Supercalifragilisticexpialidocious". (Note that this is a common technique and not unique to Disney. It is the *combination* of all the techniques we cover, in large amounts, that characterizes "Disney" music.)

- A harmonic "layering" effect. This is my term for a chord structure that is simple enough to handle two separate melodies at the same time. The song usually begins with an "A" melody and then introduces a "B" melody, sometimes a simple chorus after the verse. Then, as the song progresses, the two melodies are played at the same time. The best example of this technique is with the song, "It's a Small World (After All)". While on that ride, the careful listener can hear the chorus and the verse being sung at the same time without any need for harmonic (chordal) changes.

- A tendency to stay close to the tonic. This technique can often be mistaken for a fault in that it is usually a characteristic of simple songs, such as kids' songs or choruses. Many popular songs include a "bridge" section which usually introduces a new melodic or chordal idea. However, while they are still used, bridges are not as common with Disney music. At the risk of making Disney music sound amateur, it is important to note here that a Disney melody is often simply repeated rather than enhanced or built upon. Again, this helps to provide the pleasing and sing-able songs that make up Disney's repertoire. In addition, since much of Disney music has multiple purposes (attractions, shows, animation, etc.), it stands to reason that the flow of the song cannot be too complicated.

Rhythmic Structure

Rhythm is another tool in the Disney arsenal of musical composition. There are numerous popular songs in American culture over the years that have gained their popularity through the use of rhythmic features alone. Consider such songs as "Wipeout", "The Typewriter Song", "Baby Elephant Walk", "the *Mission Impossible* theme", and many others. Disney, of course, has used several rhythmic techniques to not only enhance their music, but once again to make it a style that is almost uniquely Disney.

One of the most common types of rhythms used in Disney music is the march. While it is natural for us to formulate a picture of "76 Trombones" marching down the street, a march is not necessarily a rhythm for parades only. In fact, a march can technically be written in any time signature and any tempo. For our purposes, however, the style being referred to is that of the standard 4/4 or 6/8 time signature with a tempo of around 120 beats per minute, though it is difficult to pin down a common tempo with Disney music. In layman's terms, we can also describe our march as the type of music that uses a lower instrument such as a tuba to provide the main beat, while another set of instruments (French horns, saxophones, strings, etc.) provides the "back beat" Most commonly, all of this "jumping around" with the beat is offset with a smoother and more relaxed melodic phrase in the higher octaves.

Disney music uses the "beat-backbeat" or "oompah" type of rhythmic feel so commonly that it has become a standard trait. Many attraction themes such as "Yo Ho, Yo Ho", "Grim, Grinning Ghosts", and "It's a Small World (After All)" take advantage of this rhythm to provide the light-hearted feel it implies. Many of the songs written by the Sherman Brothers, such as "Supercalifragilisticexpialidocious" or "Zip-A-Dee-Doo-Dah", use a variation on standard march tempos while still featuring the back beat feel.

The illustration below provides us with an excellent example of what we would expect from a Disney march. The notes in this example are not from any particular score that we are aware of. However, this music would fit as an accompaniment to dozens of Disney songs. If you are unable to read music, no worries! I'll explain soon.

In this score, the horns on the top line provide the fun little after beat that is basically a response to the bass on the bottom line, while the cellos sing along with a smooth counter melody. The bass, of course, plays the tuba-like "oompah" so prevalent in animation soundtracks. What is fascinating here is that the above clip of music (with perhaps only minor variations) could easily fit into any of the following songs (and many more besides):

- Be Our Guest
- Supercalifragilisticexpialidocious
- A Spoonful of Sugar
- Zip-a-Dee-Doo-Dah
- It's a Small World (After All)
- Heigh-Ho (It's Off to Work We Go)

Certainly there are many other rhythmic techniques used by Disney composers. After all, not every song has a march rhythm. Indeed, any of the more recent animated feature films introduce songs with a more contemporary style. Even those songs, however, tend to sound similar, though not in a bad way.

After being blown away by the Illuminations: Reflections of Earth fireworks spectacular each evening, thousands of Epcot visitors are treated to a moving rendition of "We Go On". (This would make a wonderful wedding song for anyone who may be looking!) The song is one of my favorites among the more pop or ballad Disney pieces. The rhythmic format is the standard 4/4 ballad with a dotted-quarter note/eighth note rhythm in the bass. Famous Disney songs with this type of feel include "A Whole New World", "Can You Feel the Love Tonight?", "Beauty and the Beast", and a host of others. An interesting note regarding this rhythm is that it is most often reserved for the love songs.

One final rhythmic hook takes us back to the SpectroMagic parade mentioned earlier. Since Disney has so many hit songs, it stands to reason that the parks and resorts would use these songs to their advantage as much as possible. In addition, it is a great idea to combine the songs into some sort of medley that takes the listener on a tour of Disney musicals and movies. The parade music does this in a most interesting way, and this writer was completely impressed with the overall effect.

In order to arrange a single piece that can comfortably include many different song clips, a great deal of thought needs to go into what kind of time signature to use. (A "time signature" is the numerical formula that determines the rhythmic feel of the song.) This is because a medley can become quite cumbersome if the time signature must switch back and forth constantly to accommodate the melodies. Arranger John Debney does a masterful job of this by creating a 12/8 piece that introduces a theme which is then used as filler throughout the parade. For those who do not know what a 12/8 time signature is, suffice it to say that this type of meter is unique in that it can blend well with songs of several different time signatures simultaneously. As a result, every float can carry its own theme song while blending perfectly with the overall theme. The end result is astounding and worthy of Disney music, to be sure. Many readers will recognize the opening "On this magic night" lyrics which sound quite a bit like a waltz. Amazingly enough, however, several more songs, including some from *The Little Mermaid, Snow White, Fantasia,* and others, all blend together in a wonderful array of hits, thus providing more of the "comfort music" we subconsciously long for.

Once again, at the risk of repeating myself too many times, I must mention the all-important disclaimer that these techniques are not exclusive to Disney music. Indeed, one hears music like this all the time and in many different contexts. The key here is that this is just another of the common features of Disney music that, when combined with the others we've discussed, gives Disney music its own unique flavor.

CHAPTER SIX

The Magic of Musical Consistency

Yes, we are back to this topic once again. When discussing the hooks inherent in most Disney music, consistency ranks among the most important as it allows anyone who hears a Disney song the confidence to say, "That is Disney." The consistency, however, is a product both of the hooks we've mentioned so far, and also the all-important fact that over the years only a relatively small number of composers have been used. By default, of course, this leads to consistency, even at the risk of making all songs sound alike.

There is a vast difference, though, between consistency and sameness. A composer is bound to his/her own creativity and imagination, and must always create something that reflects their inner musical mind. No matter how much of a genius a composer could be, there is always a set of characteristics in their music that will give it away as their own. Even Bach's compositions are easily identified by the first-year college music appreciation student. The key is that when music is of the highest quality, listeners anticipate and appreciate those features that separate the composer from all others.

This brings us to two of the most famous of Disney musical composers. No book of any kind on Disney music could be complete without at least a paragraph or two on the famous Sherman Brothers. Since the recent documentary on their lives, much is now known about the trials and triumphs they faced.

From a musical point of view, we cannot discuss consistency without analyzing songs from these two geniuses.

First of all, the list of contributions to Disney music from the Sherman Brothers is quite long. They were responsible for the entire score of many great Disney films such as *Mary Poppins, The Jungle Book, The Aristocats,* and *Bedknobs and Broomsticks.* Their contributions to theme park music was also extensive and included great themes from attractions such as the Carousel of Progress, Journey into Imagination, The Great Movie Ride, Walt Disney's Enchanted Tiki Room, The Many Adventures of Winnie the Pooh, and of course, "it's a small world".

Their music, to great degree, contains many of the hooks we've already discussed in this book. As with all great composers, however, the greatness of their music is beyond a complete analysis. They became famous for creating new words that the world would never forget, such as "gratifaction" from the film *Tom Sawyer.* The most famous of these words, of course, is "supercalifragilisticexpialidocious". (Disney music has always been known for great words—remember Bibbidi-Bobbidi-Boo?) They also have drawn acclaim for matching lyrics and melody with a talent equaled perhaps only by Rodgers and Hammerstein. Most important, however, is that their music truly brings out the personalities of those singing in a way that creates a wonderful bond between listener and singer.

(By the way, the Sherman Brothers also wrote the marvelous musical score to *Chitty, Chitty Bang Bang.* As great as that music is, to me it still does not seem like "Disney" music. What makes the difference? Perhaps we've all been brainwashed by some magic potion from the wicked stepmother? Or perhaps the composers are brainwashed by the ghost of Walt Disney at the moment they are hired to create a Disney piece? One may never know.)

A thought-provoking fact regarding Disney composers is that there is such a small list. When one considers the sheer volume of music coming from Disney films, cartoons, and theme parks, and then the number of years over which these songs have been written, it is amazing that so few composers exist.

There is probably much that can be said about the consistency of Disney music as it relates to the small number of Disney composers. One would think that the same musicians would create the same type of music again and again, and they would be correct. Why is it, though, that songs written by different composers in different time periods and in different styles all seem to sound like Disney songs? As mentioned earlier, one very good reason could be that the newly hired composers invested large amounts of their time listening to earlier Disney music to get a feel for what they should sound like. Another reason has to be Walt Disney himself, though after December of 1966 he was no longer around to approve or disapprove music.

The better question we must ask in this context is whether a song that strayed from Disney characteristics would be accepted among Disney purists. It is my opinion that the songs would most likely be rejected or, at the very least, not as popular. What comes to mind is a Walt Disney World Cinderella Castle birthday cake transformation in 1996 that was met with less than enthusiastic reaction among those who would prefer the castle was left alone. To stray from the norm was completely out of the question for most and simply annoying for others. Why ruin a good thing? If it ain't broke, don't fix it.

As a result, though there are some notable exceptions, most Disney music will continue to sound like Disney music has always sounded. Supporting evidence has appeared recently in some of the Broadway musicals of Disney animated films. *Beauty and the Beast*, for example, uses some different songs on Broadway than are used in the movie. Yes, they are written by the same composer, and yes, they could have been edited out of the film for time reasons, but when one examines these songs closely, it is clear that the songs don't have the same Disney feel that the others do. "Human Again" and "Maison Des Lunes" are songs that stray from the original formula in several significant ways, and are not part of the original film.

For those of you who are in complete disagreement, keep in mind that Disney does nothing at all these days without paying homage to the almighty dollar sign. Walt Disney himself cared so little about money that he nearly bankrupted the company on several occasions. Today, however, the mood is quite different and nothing is presented to the public without a significant amount of groundwork and study as to whether it will make a profit. If the Disney "feel" is what sells Disney songs, than one can be sure every song will use a similar formula, no matter who the composer or arranger may be.

What exactly is consistent about the music? We've already discussed that only a few musicians are Disney composers and we've discussed the hooks that they all seem to use. In addition to these things, there are also significant consistencies with the instrumentation and choral arranging. For example, there is a strong tendency to use choral music as a background, even in a day when choral music is not all that popular. Consider the high soprano parts in much of the Disney animation music, as well as the 4-part choir accompaniments to Disney solos. Choral music has always been a well-known feature of Disney movies and cartoons. There are few that can forget the choir as it begins the phrases of "You Can Fly" in *Peter Pan*, It is fascinating that, other than those for education, liturgy, or worship, Disney seems to have the only writers and arrangers that can get away with the use of choral music as a regular practice and attract large audiences at the same time.

The consistencies with instrumentation are equally notable. Even though Walt took many risks regarding orchestration, especially with *Fantasia*, he always returned to the familiar brass and string emphasis that marks most Disney music. Unlike pop music, of course, Disney instrumentation usually involved an entire symphonic score, and a departure from those instruments was rare, even for themed attraction sound tracks. This use of instrumentation is another thing that would set Disney music apart from other sound tracks. While pop music continues to make use of smaller and smaller combinations of instruments, Disney uses the entire orchestra regularly. This is appreciated by music lovers.

Finally, there is a consistency with the "psychological" effects of Disney music. While it is difficult to explain, all musical structure is known to have a certain psychological effect on its listeners. While most experts in this field of study can verify that this is the case, it seems very few are agreed on how or why it happens. After years of performing, most musicians can tell how a song would affect a listener by the key the song is written in. Remember that a song is always based on a particular "note" that is the "home" note to come back to. This is called the "key" of the song. Each key can have its own mood. Indeed, books have been written about keys themselves and some authors have gone far enough to assign moods to keys, as in this abridged, translated snippet from Christian Schubart's *Ideen zu einer Aesthetik der Tonkunst* (1806):

C major
Pure, with a character of innocence and simplicity.

C minor
Both love and lamentation. A longing for love.

Db major
An unusual key, that smirks rather than laughs, and devolves into grief and rapture.

D major
Triump, victory, and Hallelujah. This is often the key of marches and holiday songs.

D minor
Melancholy.

D# minor
Distress, despair, and depression. Gloom and fear.

Eb major
Love and devotion.

E major
Laughter, delight, and joy.

F major
Calm.

F minor
Funereal depression and misery. A desire for death.

F# major
Relief at difficulty overcome. The successful end of struggle.

F# minor
Resentment and discontent.

G major
Gentle, idyllic, and lyrical. A peaceful, calm key.

G minor
Dread and uneasiness, leading to dislike.

Ab major
Death and decay.

Ab minor
Struggle, with no hope of success.

A major
Innocence, cheer, and hope.

A minor
Tenderness and piety.

Bb major
Hope and confidence for better times ahead.

Bb minor
A surly, mocking key.

B major
Wild passion, from rage and jealousy to despair.

B minor
Patience and submission.

There are different explanations, of course, as to how the mind is affected by music. The emotions that Schubart associated with the keys is his take on it, though others usually come up with similar characteristics for each key.

Most fascinating is that nearly all of the Disney songs ever written fit into these characteristics. This could be a result of simple composer knowledge, or perhaps even a subconscious desire to hear a song in a certain key. Whatever the cause, it having occurred in a similar manner over so many decades is quite notable.

For whatever reason, many of the Disney songs are written in the first 3 major "flat" keys. These are the keys of F, Bb, and Eb. One quick glance at the characteristics above will reveal that these keys represent love, hope, joy, peace, and related emotions. There are some interesting exceptions to this rule. "Supercalifragilisticexpialidocious" is written in the key of C major, which is a very appropriate key. (The song "Do Re Mi" by Rodgers and Hammerstein has a very similar feel and is also written in the key of C.) Usually, the Disney songs that are written in the sharp keys represent a happy or aggressive feel. One example of this is the opening song for *Beauty and the Beast* which introduces Belle. This song is set in a small French provincial town and involves a bunch of the townspeople as they greet Belle in the morning. The song is written in the key of D and provides the perfect bright tones necessary to start off the movie.

One could spend hours and hours speculating on why keys present moods as they do. It is truly a fascinating study and there is no doubt that Disney music takes advantage of the phenomenon. What is puzzling is whether or not the composers actually had this in mind when writing. I believe that it is not a conscious decision on the composer's part, but more of an ear tuned to what sounds correct in presenting a specific mood. (There is also some thought given to the vocal range of the soloist when considering a key.) While we cannot be sure how much of this mystery applies to the popularity of a song, we can surmise that a song written in the "wrong" key could fall short of expectations if it does not set the proper mood to match its lyrics.

If one were to sit down and analyze Disney music to determine why it is what it is, consistency would have to be a major component, if not the entire key to familiarity. When anything is the same year after year, it begins to gain a reputation for being the representative of its field. While change can be a great thing, it can also harm a product in extreme ways. Remember the "New Coke" formula that experienced such failure? On the other hand, can anyone fault McDonald's for never changing their business practices and remaining consistent through the years? There are many large businesses that owe their success to consistency. Nearly everyone can close their eyes and tell someone where the electronics department is in a Walmart store. Why? Because Walmart has been so consistent in setting up their stores and one rarely sees any changes, no matter what part of the country you're in. Consistency is the name of the game, and it is definitely a large factor (perhaps the largest) in making Disney music sound like Disney music.

After all the rides and shows, one of my favorite things to do is relax, get a hot dog at Caseys, and go out on the patio to listen to Ragtime Jim. While the songs coming from Jim's little white upright piano aren't "Disney" songs per se, the exuberance is unmistakably Disney. Jim always has time to talk to his audience and then burst out with "The Entertainer" for the millionth time. He never seems to tire of it. It makes me feel like I'm transported back to Small Town USA where life is simple and innocent once again, Where little boys play pick-up games of softball and girls spin their hula hoops while their moms chat nearby.
FB / Georgia

CHAPTER SEVEN

Disney Music's Magical Quality

Henry Ford once said: "Quailty means doing it right when no one is looking."

Many would argue that the number one reason Disney parks are as popular as they are is that they pay attention to detail. Over the years, Disney parks and resorts have earned the reputation for being the most detail-oriented in the world, and the bottom line would seem to support it. Quality is a direct descendent of attention to detail. One cannot pay attention to the smallest of details without noticing and then repairing any flaws in quality of workmanship or materials.

While some may claim that Disney quality has fallen off over recent years, the same cannot be said for Disney music. There are certainly more genres that Disney has ventured into, but the popularity and complexity of Disney music continues to amaze, and sell! (There are certain critics of Disney pop music such as the songs from *High School Musical* who claim that Disney is cheapening their music and taking part in the simplistic and unoriginal teenage songs that lack any creativity. While some of that may be true, there is no one that can deny that the production quality and the choreography continues to rank near the top.)

There are many books written specifically about the attractions at Disney parks and the trivia behind these attractions. Many of those books reveal secret details about the attractions and how to find them. When one considers that these secrets exist, however, it boggles the mind that Disney would think to include them when it was simply not necessary. One example of this is in the Tower of Terror at Disney's Hollywood Studios. The bulletin board in the lobby of the hotel has a series of letters which have fallen off. The letters, however, have formed themselves into a warning: "evil tower U R doomed". What is fascinating about this detail is that 99% of all visitors to this attraction will never have a clue that it exists. Yet Disney Imagineers felt it was necessary to include it. Of course, many more Disney visitors are aware of the "hidden Mickeys" all over the parks, and especially at Epcot. These little details were hardly worth the effort. Were they?

The point is that the extra effort necessary to take care of these things contributes to the overall quality of Disney parks. Disney continues to amaze because they care about quality and it shows in everything they do. It's the same for music. But why would this be considered a hook?

Anyone who has been to a Candlelight Processional at Epcot during Christmas can testify that the quality of this performance is amazing. Even though the choirs involved are not necessarily Disney, the arrangements, the orchestra, the herald trumpets, and the staging are magnificent, and it's a performance that should not be missed by anyone. The draw (hook), however, is more than that it is simply Christmas music being performed in a theme park. The hook is quality.

My wife and I are fans of Steven Curtis Chapman and we anxiously awaited our first Candlelight Processional because we knew he would be the celebrity guest for the evening. We did not know what to expect and we assumed there would be a small concert with him singing some of his most popular songs. Instead, we were treated to him simply reading the Christmas story directly from the Bible. There were no hit songs, no Chapman band members, and no arrangements of his music. We did not hear one of our favorite singers sing. We loved the concert. It was possibly the best Christmas concert we had ever heard.

Why didn't they take advantage of the Grammy Award winning singer they had on the stage? Because they didn't need to!

Quality provides the extra ingredient necessary to make anything appealing to a large audience. It is the reason that year after year Disney parks top the attendance figure statistics for the theme parks worldwide. With Disney music, there is no question that quality is emphasized. The instrumentalists, vocalists, writers, arrangers, and AV technicians are all at the top of their game, and this is definitely by design.

Disney music is very uplifting and fun. It leaves you in a good mood and fits the environment well. I especially like the music in Epcot—they really do a good job of introducing you to the different cultures through music.
AD / Florida

CHAPTER EIGHT

Magical Musical Highlights

What follows is a slightly subjective overview of the best songs and entertainers from Disney's movie, television, and resort repertoire. Topics for this list are chosen mostly from an unofficial popularity survey taken over a period of several years, while many have been chosen simply because they are among my own favorites. The intent is to provide some interesting, if trivial information for each item and perhaps some opinion as to why it should be listed among the best. In addition, where appropriate, commentary is added.

The Ballad of Davy Crockett

What do Michael J. Fox and Davy Crockett have in common? Those of us who enjoyed the *Back to the Future* films may remember a couple of quick references to the Davy Crockett phenomenon, one of them a juke box playing "The Ballad of Davy Crockett", and the other a character in the film wearing a coonskin hat. In the year 1955, the popularity of Davy Crockett was so immense as to make it difficult for Disney to keep coonskin hats in stock. Children all over the world were considering Davy as their hero, while faithfully clearing everything on their schedule to watch each weekly episode.

In the 1950s, it was thought unwise (and perhaps even dishonorable) to mix the film industry with television. Nevertheless,

Walt Disney saw the potential of television and began producing programming that would support the studio and, ultimately, the building of Disneyland. The television series *Davy Crockett* aired its first telecast on December 15, 1954, and became an instant hit all over the United States and, eventually, the world.

"The Ballad of Davy Crockett" (the show's theme song) was actually sung by Fess Parker, the actor who portrayed the title character. Some historians claim that the first show was a bit too short for the TV time slot. As a result, George Bruns (music) and Thomas Blackburn (lyrics) were asked to write a quick musical number to fill the time. That "quick musical number" ended up taking the world by storm.

Be Our Guest

In the early 20th century, musical performers often got their start on a vaudeville stage. While considered a step below the professional level, vaudeville held its own while filling an entertainment niche throughout the country. At the same time, vaudeville-style variety programs on a much higher level were gaining the attention of the biggest stars and at the most well-known venues, such as the various theaters on Broadway. The programs often featured lavishly-costumed chorus girls who were known to perform elaborate choreography with large stage props such as staircases and sets modeled after city streets. The Ziegfeld Follies (modeled after the famed Folies Bergere in Paris) was the most popular of these programs.

Just a few years later, the film industry would take advantage of this popularity and produce grand numbers on huge soundstages such as the *Footlight Parade* production of "By a Waterfall" that used a very large number of chorus girls who formed geometric shapes viewed from various angles. The producer of this show, Busby Berkeley, used this "kaleidoscopic" choreography to his advantage on many occasions. (Another such production was a number from *Dames* in 1934.)

The genius of the Ashman/Menken song "Be Our Guest" from the movie *Beauty and the Beast* is often lost on those who are not aware of this history. Not only was the story based in France (where these productions originated), but the food chorus line effect was a nod to the famed productions of the past. Of course, the melody itself is truly memorable and the lyrics are delightfully humorous. Indeed, the most common dessert requested at the Be Our Guest restaurant at Walt Disney World's Magic Kingdom is the "grey stuff" referred to just a single time in the song. The French candelabra (Lumière) puts on his best Maurice Chevalier impression and brings down the house with his energetic dinner invitation to Belle. At the same time, the choreography of the various enchanted objects in the background is unusually mesmerizing for something that is animated.

Beauty and the Beast

It is difficult to imagine the film *Beauty and the Beast* as being in trouble and on the verge of never being produced. In fact, the film was not intended to be a musical and Walt Disney himself attempted several times to create an animated feature of the traditional fairy tale during the film-rich period between the 1930s and the 1950s. Finally, in 1989, the studio tried once again, but was overruled by then Disney chairman Jeffrey Katzenberg, who decided that the film should be a musical. (Since *The Little Mermaid* had just earned big dollars, the chairman obviously considered the musical format to be a winner.) Of course, studio politics such as this caused quite a stir and the assigned director, Richard Purdum, resigned. The final directors were Gary Trousdale and Kirk Wise and, as we all now know, the musical composer was Alan Menken and the lyrics were written by Howard Ashman who died of AIDS shortly before the film's release.

While the story itself is appealing, the musical score for *Beauty and the Beast* was remarkable. The "theme song" with the same title was an emotional and moving ballad sung by the "tea pot" character, Mrs. Potts. Many musicals (animated or otherwise) avoid a theme song, per se, because by definition a theme song would give much of the plot away and would therefore be difficult to place. In a sense, this song does exactly that by telling of the relationship between Belle and Beast (the main characters) and strongly hinting of their growing love for each other. On the other hand, the song is a tear-jerker and belongs exactly where it is, thus letting the audience know that the two will eventually be together. The only suspense remaining was over how this relationship would overcome some very difficult obstacles.

There is no doubt about the quality of this song, and the numerous awards it earned only confirm the obvious. Among these awards were the Golden Globe, Oscar, Grammy, Record of the Year, Song of the Year, and the list goes on. One interesting side note is that Disney asked Celine Dion to record the song as a single. In those days, Celine Dion was known mostly in Canada and was relatively unknown in the United States. The recording of "Beauty and the Beast" is often credited as being the one single that catapulted Dion's career.

Can You Feel the Love Tonight?

Some of the most interesting back stories relating to the Disney musicals involve the numerous discussions (even arguments) about what type of songs should be included, who should be singing them, and at what point they should be sung. As an audience, we see the final product and simply assume that what we see was the intention all along. In reality, most of the Disney musicals go through several generations of changes before the final version hits the theaters. The movie *The Lion King* was certainly no exception.

It is quite fortunate that Elton John won his argument regarding the song "Can You Feel the Love Tonight?" The original intent was to have the song sung by Timon and Pumbaa (comical characters in the film) which would give it a completely different emotion and most likely destroy its powerful effect. Elton John argued that the song should be a love ballad and the result was an Oscar-winning tune that became a fan favorite far beyond the movie itself. In addition, the song won a Grammy and a Golden Globe Award for best original song.

The song carries with it many of the hooks we discussed earlier. The melody and rhythm are filled with the sequencing techniques, while the soft rock style provides a relaxing background. Most importantly, the song presents a major part of the plot in that it shows a strong relationship between two major characters.

Dapper Dans

One of the biggest complaints about the Disney parks is that the admission prices are too high. When the average consumer makes price comparisons in their mind, they often think "amusement park" and wonder why anyone would pay so much to be "amused" for just a single day. Their mistake is to forget about the value they receive once they are inside a Disney park.

The Dapper Dans are one of the best examples of free, high-quality entertainment. While they usually make their home on Main Street, U.S.A., one never knows where they will show up at the parks in Anaheim, Orlando, Paris, or Hong Kong. Holding true to Walt Disney's desire to portray an early American small town atmosphere, the Dapper Dans will often be found singing their Barbershop style in the Main Street Barbershop where real haircuts are given to Disney guests. The Disneyland Dapper Dans are often seen on a bicycle built for four, singing as they pedal up and down Main Street, U.S.A.

Consisting of twelve performers, the quartet sings 60 or more times each week, delighting street audiences with their humor and high quality harmonies. They are usually found wearing brightly colored striped vests and matching straw hats, though they will sometimes don special costumes for various occasions. They have become so well-known that it is not unusual to see (or hear) them in performance in non-Disney environments such as television. One of the most memorable of these performances occurred when they provided the vocals for a barbershop quartet starring Homer Simpson in one of *The Simpsons* episodes.

A Dream Is a Wish Your Heart Makes

When famed German composer Franz Liszt was just 15 years old, he wrote a set of simple piano exercises (etudes). These exercises would eventually be revised over a period of 30 years, but the ideas remained consistent. The "Transcendental Etudes", as they are known, are twelve compositions known today as some of the greatest pieces written for piano. Etude #9 is called "Ricordanza" and it contains a small melody with which we are all familiar.

"A Dream is a Wish Your Heart Makes" is based on this Liszt etude. Some of the greatest of Disney songs are based on themes from classical music and, in a strange sort of way, they help to revive these great musical masterpieces for a generation of people who would not otherwise recognize them.

It is not unusual, of course, for a Disney song to refer to dreams or wishes. Indeed, it seemed like Walt's favorite theme, and one that he lived out every day of his life. When the animated movie *Cinderella* was produced in 1950, composers Mack David, Al Hoffman, and Jerry Livingston were no doubt told to expound on this theme, and it is the biggest reason we include it here, though the song itself is a great work.

It is important to distinguish the difference between a dream as something that occurs during sleep, and a dream that is something people long for and work toward. Certainly this song refers to the latter. Walt Disney was constantly hopping from one dream to another. It was no secret that once he accomplished something, he would rarely go back to it for revision. Instead, he would move on to his next dream with confidence that it would someday come true.

(By the way, Ilene Woods was the voice of Cinderella and the performer of this song in the film. She was chosen by Walt Disney over more than 300 others who auditioned for the role. As a result, she was named a Disney Legend in 2003.)

Epcot's Fountain of Nations

It seems a shame that most guests at Epcot will leave the park without even realizing that there is a wonderful, musical show at the center of Future World. To those scurrying off to find a place in line at *Soarin'* or *Test Track*, the large fountain they pass is simply a decorative obstacle in their way. Few people realize the significance of the fountain for both musical entertainment and Disney history.

Each day since Epcot's opening ceremony, its fountain has delighted guests with shows every 15 minutes. The computer-controlled dancing waters are synchronized to specially selected musical accompaniments. Many guests have discovered the secret of finding a bench nearby and choosing to rest weary feet to a wonderful program.

One interesting note is that one of the designers of the original fountain was a civil engineer who later founded a company called WET Design. Mark Fuller eventually became the famed designer of the fountains at the Bellagio Hotel in Las Vegas.

Fantasmic!

One of the most crowd-pleasing highlights of visiting a Disney park is the "kiss goodnight" that comes in various forms, depending on the park. Most of these nightly performances contain some combination of live actors, fireworks, water effects, projections, lighting effects, lasers, and, of course, music, making it a fan favorite.

Feed the Birds

At the risk of too much speculation, and perhaps too much religion, allow me to offer an opinion of Walt Disney's spiritual life. It was plain for everyone to see that Walt was essentially a humanist. By this I mean that his thoughts and ideas always came back to a central theme that the solutions to man's problems are within the mind and heart of man himself. His philosophies (most evident with his EPCOT ideas) focused on providing perfect communities that would by their very design eliminate most crime and poverty. For Walt, environment was the key and his ultimate goal was to design and create a utopian society to prove this idea.

When the Sherman Brothers presented the song "Feed the Birds" to Walt Disney for the first time, he knew it was a song that would have crucial meaning both to the film *Mary Poppins*, for which it was written, and to his own life.

There have been numerous opinions offered as to what Walt truly believed regarding spirituality and religion. While Walt acknowledged the existence of a God, he rarely (if ever) went to church and never spoke of an afterlife. Walt's life and philosophies truly seemed to be summed up in this simple song and the scene of a beggar woman selling seeds to feed the birds.

Festival of the Lion King

For years now, my favorite musical performance has been *The Festival of the Lion King*. The show is a high-energy, fun-filled overview of the film *The Lion King*, with enough eye candy to keep even those who have seen it multiple times finding new features at each performance. It can be seen at Disney's Animal Kingdom at Walt Disney World, and in Adventureland at Hong Kong Disneyland.

The show features the great songs from the Elton John/Tim Rice movie score in a revue format that does not provide a plot or summary of the film itself. Instead, the celebratory style keeps the audience involved by assigning animal names to sections of the theater and encouraging those in each section to make appropriate animal noises at selected times.

As with all Disney entertainment, the soloists in this one have wonderful voices and truly amaze the audience with their talent. At the same time, an eclectic array of "side shows" include stilt walkers, floats with Audio-Animatronic animals, acrobatic monkeys, and dancing birds.

The Festival of the Lion King recently moved to a new theater in the Africa section of Disney's Animal Kingdom. This was due to the construction of Avatar Land and the need to replace the Camp Minnie-Mickey area of the park.

Firehouse Five Plus Two

The significance of this well-known Dixieland band is much more than musical, though they certainly were popular for musical reasons. The band's leader, Ward Kimball, was the animator who created Jiminy Cricket. Kimball also had a very interesting home life that included a full-size locomotive in his back yard. His hobbies did not end with trains, however, and his love for jazz music often resulted in lunch-time jam sessions in his office at the Disney studio. He has told the story about studio musicians playing along with records and then discovering that they actually sounded great when the recording stopped.

A few of the band members (along with Kimball) became famous for their "day jobs", most notably Frank Thomas who went on to become one of history's greatest animators and one of Disney's famed Nine Old Men. The voice of Mickey Mouse, Jim McDonald, played drums, and Harper Goff, designer of the *Nautilus* in the movie *20,000 Leagues Under the Sea* (among many other projects), played banjo.

When the band was asked to be part of a Horseless Carriage Club, they found an old fire truck and donned firemen uniforms for the gig. The name "Firehouse Five Plus Two" was given simply because they had seven members at the time. Their music caught on quickly and they ended up making quite a name for themselves as jazz musicians, despite the fact that Kimball claims they never rehearsed.

The band stood as a symbol of camaraderie among studio personnel, despite the many problems that had occurred as a result of strikes and overall studio strife during the 1940s. While Walt Disney did not refer to them often, he was fond of their music and used it in Disney productions, including the Goofy cartoon *How to Dance*.

Grand Floridian Society Orchestra

There are many Disney parks fans (my wife and I included) that have visited so often they know the many secrets of enjoying the most while paying the least. Walt Disney World, for example, hides many wonderful secrets for those who want to spend very little money and still have a great time. Some would even suggest that the "free" activities are just as enjoyable as those which cost the proverbial arm and leg.

One such activity involves a free concert in an environment that is definitely "high society". (It is difficult to give this information away because of the potential for divulging too much and bringing an end to the secret!) An evening trip to the Grand Floridian at Walt Disney World can summon up the "Great Gatsby" in all of us as we enter the overlap of the Victorian Age and the Roaring Twenties. The architecture of the resort brings to mind the great Florida beach resorts of the past, and the first view of the five-story lobby continues to provoke oohs and aahs among guests.

There are several methods for accessing this hotel without the need to mortgage the homestead. One of the easiest is to park at Downtown Disney (soon to be "Disney Springs") and hop on the next bus to the resort. Upon arrival, the entertainment options are many, including shopping in the lobby, walking out to the pier on the lagoon (perhaps staying late enough to view the Wishes fireworks show), or finding a comfortable seat near the large grand piano at the center. The piano is played often and the pianist enjoys taking your requests. However, one of the most delightful attractions of the lobby has to be the Grand Floridian Society Orchestra that plays a couple of sets each evening. They are located on the second floor balcony and their big band, jazz, swing, and Disney numbers can be heard throughout the lobby area.

One listen to this orchestra will reveal the talent of these musicians led by drummer Patrick Doyle. Like the piano player in the lobby, the band often takes requests, and like the Main Street Philharmonic, their repertoire is huge. One of the best ways to enjoy this band is to grab a chair in the lounge just behind them in the balcony area. Munch on some appetizers and enjoy a beverage while taking in their concert just a few feet away.

Grim Grinning Ghosts

When one thinks of the highlights of a theme park attraction, it is not often that the theme song comes to mind. On the other hand, when the attraction is a Disney attraction, what could be considered a minor detail is usually significant.

Back in the early days of Disneyland, Walt asked Xavier Atencio to write the "script" for the Pirates of the Caribbean attraction, and when turned out to be successful, tapped him to write the theme song for the Haunted Mansion, as well. "Grim, Grinning, Ghosts" accompanies guests at the Mansion and then in their minds on the way home from the park.

Atencio created solid hits on his first attempts, something established musicians have a hard time accomplishing. He also had a part in several other attractions, including Adventure Thru Inner Space, If You Had Wings, Space Mountain, Spaceship Earth, World of Motion, and the Mexico Pavilion at Epcot.

From a musical standpoint, "Grim Grinning Ghosts" has some interesting chordal structures that make it perfect for playing at almost any tempo and with many different types of instrumentation. For example, the song can be heard with just sustained organ chords in the "stretching room" at the beginning of the ride. As a person progresses through the mansion, however, the song begins to add tempo and instrumentation until, in the final graveyard scene, the tempo is spirited (pun intended) and numerous instruments and voices are fully involved. This type of music writing takes plenty of forethought and imagination, something that is quite common among Disney musicians.

> When the crypt doors creak and the tombstones quake
> Spooks come out for a swingin' wake
> Happy haunts materialize, and begin to vocalize,
> Grim grinnin' ghosts come out to socialize
> Now don't close your eyes and don't try to hide
> Or a silly spook may sit by your side
> Shrouded in a daft disguise, they pretend to terrorize,
> Grim grinnin' ghosts come out to socialize
> As the moon climbs high o'er the dead oak tree

>Spooks come out for the midnight spree
>Creepy creeps with eerie eyes, start to shriek and harmonize
>Grim grinnin' ghosts come out to socialize!
>When you hear the knell of a requiem bell
>Weird glows gleam where spirits dwell
>Restless bones etherealize, rise as spooks of every size
>(maniacal laughter)
>If you would like to join our jamboree
>There's a simple rule that's compulsory:
>Mortals pay a token fee, rest in peace, the hauntings free,
>So hurry back, we would like your company!

The challenge is to ride through the Haunted Mansion and NOT come out of it humming this song. As a musician, I often find myself humming the chords incessantly. Perhaps that is the best indicator of musical quality.

Heigh Ho (It's Off to Work We Go)

The significance of *Snow White and the Seven Dwarfs* cannot be overstated for the film world in general and for Disney fans in particular. Frank Churchill wrote the music for the film and Larry Morey wrote the lyrics, while Paul Smith and Leigh Harline contributed to the incidental music. (Morey was one of the film's directors in addition to his musical duties.) The movie is listed in the American Film Institute's 100 greatest American films, and the music was given an Oscar nomination for Best Musical Score. (*Snow White and the Seven Dwarfs* was the first American film to have a soundtrack album released with the film.)

Originally intended to focus on the dwarfs, the movie turned out to be a bit darker, a bit more sinister than expected, with an emphasis on the relationship between Snow White and the Queen. However, the scenes featuring the dwarfs were sufficient enough to give the audience a look at the serious side of these otherwise comical men. Their work ethic, something that was important to Walt Disney, was evident throughout the film, but never more so than while singing this song and marching toward the mine.

There is an interesting modern philosophical application to the song that is rather depressing. Indeed, if the song didn't have such a rollicking and joyful melody/rhythm combination, the song could be interpreted as a dirge. Consider the following lyric from the second verse:

> We dig up diamonds by the score
> A thousand rubies, sometimes more
> But we don't know what we dig 'em for
> We dig dig dig a-dig dig

Some who have over-analyzed the song point out the futility of the hard work and the necessity to whistle for a small if futile amount of encouragement. Could this be true? Did Walt see this in the lyrics and try to make a subtle point about life and work? The world will never know.

Hoop-Dee-Doo Musical Revue

In the world of entertainment, longevity is everything. The quality of a Broadway show is often measured by the number of weeks it has been playing. The quality of a film is often measured by the length of time it takes to get to a second-run theater. It's really quite simple—when the crowds keep coming, the show keeps going.

The Hoop Dee-Doo Musical Revue has been delighting audiences for over 40 years and there is no sign that it will be stopping any time soon. The vaudeville, hoe-down style is simple, but pleasing. The comedy is often corny and dry. The music itself is of basic construction and performed well. The food is tasty and the all-you-can-eat bonus is certainly a treat. But nothing really stands out as exceptional.

So what makes it so popular?

Like everything else at a Disney park, the most effective ingredient to popularity is the attraction's ability to transport a guest into another world at another time. One can listen to fun music, or eat chicken any time, but to be vaulted to a barn in the middle of the countryside, with authentic scenery and a cast of characters that live their parts every second is to be truly entertained.

Since this popular show is located at the Fort Wilderness campground, getting to it can be difficult. One option is to take water transportation from the Transportation and Ticket Center, the Magic Kingdom, or any of the monorail loop resorts. Another option is to wait at the entrance to Fort Wilderness for a bus that will traverse the campground itself and eventually drop you off at a long, yet manageable walk to the theater.

Despite the difficulty of getting there, the isolated nature of the show adds to the notion that the real world (and all of its problems) has been left behind for an evening of fantasy and fun.

I Wan'na Be Like You

Most people know that the film *The Jungle Book* was Walt Disney's last film project before his death on December 15, 1966. The film opened just 10 months after Walt's death to rave reviews and a significant studio profit. As with many of the Disney films, the story itself does not necessarily match the original and is much lighter and more family-oriented. Rudyard Kipling's *The Jungle Book* was far darker and scarier then what appeared on the Disney screen.

Another in a long list of Sherman Brothers creations, this song perfectly accomplishes Walt Disney's goal of adding a lighthearted and comical mood where the story would otherwise be distressing and bleak. The Sherman Brothers were experts at this task and, in fact, caused quite a stir with the author of *Mary Poppins* (P.L. Travers) when they attempted to do the same thing to her story. Travers preferred reality over fantasy and resented any attempts to lighten the mood.

More significant, however, is that this song is among the last that Walt Disney had any role in creating. It was Walt's decision, in fact, that led to the Sherman Brothers involvement in the first place, as the songs originally written for the score by Terry Gilkyson were not "happy enough" to lighten up the film. When the Shermans were asked, Walt specifically requested that they find the scarier spots and add a fun song for an emotional counter-balance. The wisdom of his decision, whether one would agree artistically or not, was confirmed at the box office.

Illuminations

Many Walt Disney World fans that live in Florida are familiar with a lightly traveled toll way to the west of the parks (Route 429). They are also familiar with a certain "higher ground" location on this road that is the perfect spot for driving (or stopping at the side of the road) around 9 pm each evening. The vantage point allows views of the skies over all 4 parks and, in particular, the fireworks from Wishes at the Magic Kingdom and Illuminations at Epcot, happening at the same time. (On rare occasions, the fireworks from Fantasmic! can also be seen, but more often the times do not match up.) The differences between the shows are more evident from this distance, and it soon becomes obvious that Illuminations was meant for a closer audience, while Wishes was meant to be seen from far away.

In any case, the shows are the highlight of the day for all guests and the Epcot performance of Illuminations (from a lagoon-side location) can easily take your breath away. At one time, the cost for each show was estimated at over $25,000, and this is not surprising when considering the technology: lasers, a propane "inferno barge" that uses 400 gallons of propane per show, and fireworks that are among the most technologically advanced in the world. (Each shell contains a computerized timing chip to be sure that the explosion is perfectly timed.) The system used to launch the fireworks features a special compressed-air system that ensures a perfect altitude (and a quiet launch) for each shell.

It is important to remember that Disney is all about story and speaks little about technology. The show itself symbolizes the creation of planet Earth and the three acts represent Chaos, Order, and Meaning. The opening dialogue is as follows:

> Good evening. On behalf of Walt Disney World, the place where dreams come true, we welcome all of you to Epcot

and World Showcase. We've gathered here tonight around the fire, as people of all lands have gathered for thousands and thousands of years before us, to share the light and to share a story -- an amazing story, as old as time itself, but still being written. And though each of us has our own individual stories to tell, a true adventure emerges when we bring them all together as one. We hope you enjoy our story tonight: Reflections of Earth.

The music for Illuminations was composed by Gavin Greenaway in collaboration with famed *Lion King* composer Hans Zimmer. Greenaway wrote the scores for well-known films such as *Gladiator* and *Pearl Harbor*. With Illuminations, the synchronization between music and pyrotechnics is especially amazing since the music itself could stand alone as concert-quality entertainment, yet it finds even more emotion and power from a detailed choreography of fire. The music for "Reflections of Earth" became so popular that is has been used for multiple events around the world over the years.

It's a Small World (After All)

We have already discussed to some degree this song and its almost comical reputation for installing itself into people's minds. We've also reviewed its simplicity in composition and in style. What we have not examined is the true greatness of the song with regard to its meaning and the symbolic nature of the melody and chord structure. While it is entirely possible (perhaps probable) that the Sherman Brothers did not stop to think about a deep symbolism within the chords or rhythm, it is notable that one can look at how it is constructed and come away amazed at its poignant connections.

The chord structure of this song is simple enough to allow the melody of the verse to be played or sung simultaneously with the chorus, with no dissonance or rhythmic distortion. As mentioned, Walt's original intent was to have the dolls in the attraction sing the national anthems of their countries, as if standing on their own to represent their home. When it was determined that one simple song was far better for expressing a message of peace, the Sherman Brothers came up with "It's a Small World (After All)" and dolls from all over the world were able to come together as one musical unit, singing a song that in itself was capable of a peaceful harmonic and rhythmic duet.

Of course, any song that is sung by a children's choir over and over again is bound to gain a large and sympathetic audience, especially with an eye candy environment packed to the ceiling with the cute, colorful dolls, all in movement synchronized to music and appropriate for the various countries. Plus, the guests in the attraction are seated in a very low boat and looking up at the children, as if to spy on them as they were having a "good ole time" amongst their friends, without a care in the world.

JAMMitors (Epcot)

This tongue-in-cheek entry is most deserving because the act has convinced so many people that they are actually employed as janitors for Epcot. The trademark of Disney parks is that a guest is taken out of reality and firmly implanted into fantasy for the entire time of their visit. Like Belle in *Beauty and the Beast*, a guest never knows what may be around the corner. The trash cans may start singing, the trees may start dancing, and the janitors may start playing a concert.

The JAMMitors are a trio of professional percussionists made to look like every day janitors strolling around the park with their cleaning equipment. When it is time for their "break", they line up their garbage cans and begin to entertain anyone that will listen by playing the cans as if they were drums. Of course, the combination of wise-crack remarks, a wide array of goofy cleaning "instruments", and an obvious talent for music makes this concert a great way for guests to stop and relax for a while. This seemingly simple way to entertain is actually part of the major overhaul that Disney started in 1955. It was this overhaul that defines the true difference between and theme park and an amusement park.

Amusement parks were the first to appear on the scene. In fact, depending on certain interpretations, true amusement parks may have been around since the 16th century. An amusement park can be defined as a fixed location where multiple rides and attractions are assembled to entertain people. Sounds simple, doesn't it?

Over the years, however, the definition of an amusement park has been clouded by developments in ride manufacturing, the invention of the automobile and the television, and the need for entertainment to match and/or exceed the expectations of its audience. These changes have been the cause for bankruptcies and closures of many amusement parks, along with upgrades and innovations for others. One thing remained the same: the parks themselves were always just collections of attractions, no matter how disjointed or tacky looking the collection appeared.

While there is still much controversy regarding the introduction of the "theme park", most experts believe that Walt Disney was its inventor, though he was highly influenced by Knott's Berry Farm and the amusement parks of Europe. So what makes a theme park different from an amusement park?

A true "theme" park is labeled as such because it consists of different themed lands or regions within its borders. Great efforts are made to create the illusion of another world or culture using landscaping, architecture, music, food, employees, and attractions. In a theme park, the rides often take second place to the environment they are placed in. The more a park is able to take its guests out of the "real world" and into a world of fantasy, the more it can be labeled a theme park. Because Walt Disney used film directors instead of architects for the design of his park, he was able to create a true escape from reality as if the theme park were a movie on a screen.

With the opening of Walt Disney World in 1971, the next step in the evolution of the theme park took place. An upgrade of sorts happened when Disney combined the theme park with hotels, golf courses, water recreation, and (eventually) more theme parks. In a way, the theme park was a conglomeration of amusement parks, each with their own theme, and this next step was a conglomeration of theme parks. It has been suggested that we call this the "themed resort", though other terms would certainly fit.

It is quite possible, with the advent of Disney's Wide World of Sports, the sport fishing, the water sports, the gourmet dining, and the camping, that just about everything one could do on a vacation can be found in one location, thus further enhancing the step away from reality. The themed resort is a one-of-a-kind, one-stop shop for the dream vacation.

So how does this relate to the JAMMitors?

Because Epcot is basically a theme park, the goal of its designers is to keep every minute of the day filled with attractions and events that will work to distract the minds of the guests and keep them believing that they are "in a land far away" from problems and reality. The JAMMitors, the Dapper Dans, the Voices of Liberty, the Main Street Philharmonic, and many other entertainers fill in the cracks of time during the day that could allow for just enough reality to creep back. After all, if a guest doesn't have time to think about the bills, the nasty neighbor, or the clogged sink, he or she is much happier and ready to spend more of their money.

Kiss the Girl

In great contrast to what has already been said about Disney songs usually following a "formula" for success is that Disney songs do not necessarily sound alike and cover an immense variety of genres. Both can be true, of course, and the massive variety of styles among Disney songs only highlights the talents of Disney composers for writing to fit a mood or a story.

"Kiss the Girl" is a light-hearted song sung by a crab named Sebastian in the animated film *The Little Mermaid*. Its style is calypso and the lyrics are a plea by Sebastian to Prince Eric that he kiss Ariel before it is too late for her to become human. The song was nominated for an Academy Award and a Golden Globe Award for Best Original Song.

Let It Go

It is interesting that there is so much speculation about why the animated film *Frozen*, the film where this song is performed, became such a smash sensation. It is almost as if the critics are desperate, yet unable to find a reason for their positive reviews.

On the other hand, the thought-provoking lyrics for "Let It Go" must certainly be the biggest reason for its magnetism. They speak of a daughter of royalty who "played the game" for most of her life, only to lose control and reveal that there is more to who she is than meets the eye. By singing the words "Let it go", she finally gives in and breaks the bonds of superficial pretention.

Does this situation speak to more lives than one could realize? Are there thousands of fans who can relate to Elsa's desire to be "real" among friends and family? The answer is not that simple. However, it seems that a nerve has been struck and Disney will be taking advantage of the resulting profits for a long time to come.

(By the way, the Voices of Liberty perform their version of the song in a video that you can find on YouTube.)

Main Street Electrical Parade

Some of the most unnoticed, yet indispensable features of Disney parks are the background music and sound effects being played throughout. Music has a crucial role in setting the scene for each section of the park, but this must be done without it being noticed. Sound technicians create amazing effects, including the automated variation of sounds or music based on what is going on at the time. One simply cannot imagine what a visit to the Disney parks would be like without the lighthearted and playful music of Main Street, U.S.A. or the jungle music and sounds in Adventureland.

Perhaps one of the most revolutionary of the sound techniques is the ability to trigger music to match what is being seen in a parade. The Main Street Electrical Parade was the first to use radio-activated triggers that were tied to specific floats. This allowed for a magical transformation of background music as each new float entered specific zones along Main Street. This feature was seen as high-tech in its day and the principles behind its use are still considered to be ground-breaking. No matter where a guest would sit for the parade, the music and the sights would be the same, and perhaps most amazing, the transformation between various background songs was seamless, something that involves some tricky musical composition techniques.

The parade itself is an electrical menagerie of lights and characters meant to light up the night, accompanied by what could be considered a controversial style of music in the early 1970's. The parade theme song is entitled "Baroque Hoedown" and it consists of electronic synthesizer stylings similar to the early Moog arrangements from experimental composers. The sound itself was not popular at first among the Midwestern tastes often found at the Magic Kingdom, but the fit was appropriate and the sound caught on quickly.

It should be noted that the original electrical parade was constructed on top of seven barges that made their way through the Seven Seas Lagoon each evening. The same type of music was played and the effect was perfectly suited to the wide spaces between stage (barge) and audience (hotel guests along the beaches) and the need to increase volume levels appropriately. (The water version still runs today.)

The parade has seen several changes of location and floats over the years, but continues to delight the guests at Walt Disney World's Magic Kingdom each evening.

Main Street Philharmonic

Not too many years ago, my wife and I decided to do something that we had always labeled as "stupid". It was July 4 and we decided to find ourselves a great seat on the porch at the Magic Kingdom's railroad station in Walt Disney World. It was only about 2:00 in the afternoon and we intended to keep our seats all the way through the patriotic fireworks display at 10:00 pm. We purchased a deck of Mickey Mouse playing cards at the nearby souvenir store, and we made plans to take turns running for food and drinks. No matter what, we were going to have the best seats possible for the evening's events, in spite of what common sense would tell us.

Our decision was a good one, to say the least. We witnessed a fabulous fireworks presentation from a great vantage point. We also met some great people from the UK with whom we had some very interesting discussions. However, the biggest benefit of our long stay on the porch was something very unexpected.

A couple of times during the afternoon we were treated to a fantastic concert by the Main Street Philharmonic brass marching band. We had heard them many times before, but it was always in passing on Main Street or while we were heading in a different direction and focused on other things. Our advantage at this point was that we were going nowhere. As a result, we had front-row seats for some of the best music we had ever heard. Trumpet players made ultra-high notes sound like child's play. Percussionists made simple marching drums sound like 15-piece drum kits. Most important, though, was the balance and musicianship so very evident in everything they played.

One special performance was an additional bonus to our afternoon. While we knew about the 5:00 pm flag-lowering ceremony, we were not completely aware of what it involved. The ceremony was truly inspirational with the great music of the band along with the beautiful harmonies of the Dapper Dans. A veteran was chosen from the audience to not only help with the lowering of the flag, but to receive it as a gift from the park.

Of course, all of this was being witnessed from the front row of the train station's porch, directly in front of and over the top of the band as they played. What an experience! Those eight hours felt more like just one hour and we were already making plans to do the same thing the following year.

Mickey and the Magical Map

While much of the musical entertainment at the Disney parks takes advantage of the finest of musicians, it has not been known to combine that talent with the latest in technology. Indeed, most music at the parks is significantly "low tech", though that has never been a problem. *Mickey and the Magical Map* first appeared in the Fantasyland Theater at Disneyland on May 25, 2013, and its entry in this listing is based on the clever use of stage technology that blends with a wonderful musical performance.

The foundation of this show's technology is an extremely large LED screen that serves as the back drop (and "map") for Mickey's adventures as a painter. As with many good Mickey Mouse plots, something goes wrong and Mickey becomes a part of the animated map. Of course, this means that Mickey can make "stops" throughout the world, conveniently allowing for great Disney songs of various countries and cultures to be highlighted. Some of the songs include "Reflection" from *Mulan*, "Under the Sea" from *The Little Mermaid*, "I Wanna Be Like You" from *The Jungle Book*, and "Dig a Little Deeper" from *The Princess and the Frog*.

Disney Imagineers succeeded at blending technical stage craft and musical numbers without the distraction that is commonly a problem. This giant map is a wonder not just because of its high resolution and beautiful artwork, but also because of its seamless work as an element of the show. The audience accepts that Mickey morphs from real life to animation because the effect is completely realistic. As an entertainment ingredient, technology is only useful when it is known not as technology, but as a character in the performance. It is highly likely that Disney fans will be seeing much more of these techniques in future Disney entertainment.

Mickey Mouse March

Can you think of some great songs from 1955? "Blue Suede Shoes", "Folsom Prison Blues", "Let There Be Peace on Earth", "The Great Pretender", "Afternoon in Paris", and "Where Have All the Flowers Gone?" are among the most familiar. However, the one song that hit the airwaves in 1955 and continues to be a well-known hit today is the "Mickey Mouse March" as performed first on *The Mickey Mouse Club* television show.

This simple, yet fun to sing theme song was famous for its spelling out of the words "Mickey Mouse", and even today it is difficult for anyone to spell out those letters without reciting the accompanying "See you real soon." or "Why? Because we like you!" The composer, Jimmie Dodd, was a prolific writer and would write many of the songs used on the television show. In fact, there were often special days on the show known as "Theme Days" in which a new Jimmie Dodd song would be presented to represent the theme of the day.

Unfortunately, the song also conjures memories of a day when children were still allowed to be children. It is a song that reflected the philosophy of Walt Disney in that he wanted to create a world that would protect children and allow them to act their age without reprimand. For some, the tendency for Walt to alter fairy tales and legends for the sake of eliminating darkness and elevating innocence was a harmful fraud that would shield children from a necessary reality. For others, Walt was on the right track, but could never hope to accomplish his impossible dream of building a perfect society in which children would grow and learn.

Whatever one's opinion, there is no doubt of the influence that Walt Disney had on the children of his day. When *The Mickey Mouse Club* aired each week for those four years in the 1950s, children all over the world would be in their place in front of the television singing along.

The Old Mill

The true sign of quality in art is a depth of meaning that is often overlooked by the public. Those that appreciate the Disney parks, for example, do so because they have learned of the multitude of details in the architecture, the attractions, the landscaping, the music, and the overall designs. Indeed, a true connoisseur of the Disney parks will never stop learning about the details behind what they see, and they will never stop being amazed at exactly how many details there are.

The same holds true for Disney animation. *The Old Mill* is a 1937 Silly Symphony cartoon produced by Walt Disney with a musical score written by Leigh Harline. The film itself was groundbreaking in that it used the "multiplane camera" for the first time. The camera was invented by Ub Iwerks and represented a revolution in animation techniques in that it allowed for animators to create a 3D effect with motion and backgrounds.

The music for *The Old Mill* was a work of genius and often goes unappreciated. Harline uses techniques similar to Vivaldi in the *Four Seasons* concertos that so vividly represent the birds of spring, the storms of summer, and other appropriate seasonal effects. When the storm in *The Old Mill* begins to approach, the music (which incorporates melodies from Johann Strauss) becomes dramatic in its fury and continues to build in its intensity until the calm finally arrives. (All of this occurs while animals run to the mill to be protected from the storm.)

Sadly, the Disneyland representation of the Old Mill on the Storybook Land Canal Boats attraction was recently replaced by the city of Arendelle of *Frozen* fame. As the generations pass, only Disney purists consider this to be the important statement that it is. While logic maintains that parks should constantly update to relate to the current constituency, the heart finds it difficult to see Disney's historically significant symbols disappear at an alarming rate.

Pirates of the Caribbean Movie Theme

Disney music has topped the ranks of popularity in nearly every genre over several decades. However, if there were a weak spot in the portfolio of Disney music it would include the dramatic and moving symphonic movie scores such as what John Williams has made so popular with such themes as *Close Encounters of the Third Kind*, *Star Wars*, *Indiana Jones*, and *Harry Potter*.

The symphonic sound that is dominated by low brass instrumentation, with an emphasis on French horn melodic features, became such a staple with these great films that the music was nearly impossible to separate from the story. After all, one only has to hear the opening phrases of "The Imperial March" to envision storm troopers and the menacing look (and breathing) of Darth Vader.

Until the premier of the *Pirates of the Caribbean* film series, this type of theme was difficult to find. It is entirely possible that this absence would have continued were it not for a last-minute change to the music production team that resulted in the introduction of Klaus Badelt and Hans Zimmer (among others) as the chosen composers. Badelt was actually responsible for the theme itself, though the ideas for nearly all of the songs in the film came from Zimmer. Amazingly, Zimmer claims to have written most of the film's tunes in a single night and recorded them in a simply synthesizer format from which the other composers would work. (The change of musical personnel at such a late date caused all of the music production to be rushed, though no one would ever be able to distinguish it from something that took years.)

While critics gave the film score mixed reviews, the audience reviews were highly positive and, perhaps most importantly, a major step had been taken with the introduction to this type of symphonic music. Of course, the style and plot of a film determines what its theme should sound like, and the majority of Disney films were childish enough to warrant the "cutesy" and bouncy melodies that were composed. There is little room for a grand symphony as the accompaniment for *Muppets Most Wanted*, for example, or *Wreck-It Ralph*. However, as Disney continues to delve into real-life action films, it is highly possible that we will begin to hear more of the John Williams style from up-and-coming Disney composers.

Ragtime Jim (WDW Magic Kingdom)

Jim Omohundro (Ragtime Jim) has been playing piano several times a day for over 30 years at Casey's Corner in Walt Disney World's Magic Kingdom. The ragtime piano is certainly appropriate for the old-time small Midwestern town atmosphere, and the talent that Jim displays is nearly impossible to believe. I am a pianist as well and still find myself staring in awe at his fingers while he plays. Even when one considers the number of years he may have played a certain arrangement, it is still quite entertaining to see what he can do with only ten fingers. (Maybe he has twelve?)

Ragtime Jim is the true picture of what Walt envisioned as an entertainer for his parks. Not only does he have an immense amount of talent, he is able to anticipate nearly any request or any type of audience. It is only on rare occasions when Jim does not know a requested song, and when he starts to play those that he does know, the arrangements are out of this world. In addition, Jim strives to get the audience involved, even to the point of asking children to play certain notes on cue.

It is said that there are many Ragtime Jim fans that visit the Magic Kingdom simply to hear him play. If so, it seems that my previous statement about the admission being worth the price of entertainment alone stands true.

SpectroMagic

The "Kiss Good Night" feature at the Disney parks is an effective marketing tool because at a theme park the first impression is not the most important. The last impression is the most important because it is the feeling in the hearts of guests travelling home that determine whether or not they are anxious to return. A wonderful fireworks show or colorful parade goes a long way toward warming the heart of even a disappointed customer.

Without exception, but with many variations, the evening "kisses" always include a multitude of colors. Certainly the fireworks bring eye candy at its best and the parades are always those that can light up the night with millions of tiny bulbs. However, the one parade that outshines all other evening performances musically has always been SpectroMagic. This most popular parade included musical arrangements and orchestrations that truly thrilled the soul and provided goose bumps for all in attendance, especially appreciative musicians.

As mentioned earlier, the music was intricate in its composition and the magic of its tunes was worth waiting the entire day. The songs began with the words, "On this magic night..." and go on to integrate with several stories and scenes, all tied musically and thematically into the main theme. In fact, as a musician I would have been satisfied simply sitting on the curb listening to the music by itself. The Florida evenings and the colorful lights are nice, but I was always blown away by the wonderful music.

Unfortunately, SpectroMagic can now only be spoken of in the past tense. While conspiracy theories abound regarding the reason for its demise, it seems the most reliable story is that the floats were damaged while in storage. This seems hard to believe when considering the efforts taken to protect floats and holiday decorations when not being viewed by the public. Regardless, the show is no more and we must settle for the electronic music of the Main Street Electrical Parade.

Supercalifragilisticexpialidocious

The title of this song alone deserves its own place in any book on Disney music. Indeed, the Sherman Brothers were responsible for several words being added to the English dictionary, and this word has become a symbol of sorts for all things happy and the music of Walt Disney productions. In addition, the song was listed as number 36 in the American Film Institute's survey of the top songs in American cinema.

The word itself is evidently a form of common children's words from the early 20th century. According to several sources, there was a practice at the time of combining "double-talk" words to make up all sorts of fun sentences for children to converse with. Even the Sherman Brothers themselves admitted that the word was a product of their youth and it was transformed several times while they were writing the song.

In *Mary Poppins*, the song is inserted as a rather pointless, but fun tune that uses the word as "something to say when you have nothing to say". It brings to mind many well-known songs over the years that contain lyrics, themselves admitting that there are no lyrics at all. The story is told, for example, of the famous song by the band *Chicago* entitled "25 or 6 to 4". Evidently, the band members were required to write songs by certain deadlines. On the night before the deadline, band member and composer Robert Lamm could not think of anything to say. In fact, it was 25 or 26 minutes to 4am and nothing was coming to mind. The lyrics themselves speak of "wondering what I can say" and "sitting cross-legged on the floor" as he attempted to come up with some words to a song.

The point is that there are no special rules for lyrics and the sky is the limit. The Sherman Brothers were often reaching for that sky and often came up with nonsense words and phrases that ended up being a hit with children and adults alike. You know, you can say it backwards, which is "dociousaliexpilistic-fragicalirupes", but that's going a bit too far, don't you think?

That's How You Know

One sign of true musical greatness is the freedom to parody and even ridicule your own works with the result being another great work. The 2007 Disney film *Enchanted* was in itself a parody of Disney animation over the years. When a princess becomes a real-life human and enters New York City, the differences between the idealistic life of an animated princess and a real-life woman are made obvious. The film, therefore, takes advantage of this sometimes comical difference and the music follows suit with styles and choreography that are adorable.

The song "That's How You Know" answers the question, "How do you know when you're in love?" It is an amusing, yet grand musical number that takes in most of New York's Central Park and hundreds of "bystanders" as they enter into an energetic Broadway-style dance number. Of course, the comical and corny effect of having innocent and uninvolved people suddenly joining in without rehearsal is intentional and, indeed, the main male character (Patrick Dempsey) is seen rolling his eyes on numerous occasions throughout the song. Even more comical is that the numerous people who join in are not those you'd expect to find in Central Park, such as a fully-outfitted steel band, elderly people who dance, and a group of Bavarians dancing in native style.

While the song received numerous nominations and awards, perhaps its most interesting feature is that the composer (Alan Menken) was himself a Disney animated film veteran having written music for *Under the Sea* and *Beauty and the Beast*, both of which had similar "show-stopping" dance numbers.

The fantasy that this song portrays is set against the background of modern-day New York with the intention of showing the immense contrast and then laughing at the result. The scene is also reminiscent of a contemporary fad called a "flash mob" in which the same type of thing happens, with a supposedly random person beginning to sing, only to have a large group of people join in with a well-rehearsed and choreographed number. Needless to say, the surprise that this scene presents to true bystanders in a train station or shopping mall is something that they will never forget. Of course, the performers receive similar joy from what they accomplish.

There's a Great Big Beautiful Tomorrow

As this book is being written, The Carousel of Progress is celebrating its 40th anniversary at Walt Disney World. Back in the 1960s, when the Carousel of Progress was being prepared for the New York World's Fair, the Audio-Animatronic technology used to tell the story of progress was the highest tech of the day. Audiences at the fair, and subsequently at the Disney parks, would be amazed at the life-like actions of the robotic figures on stage. In addition, a theater unlike any other would transport an entire audience from scene to scene using a giant carousel.

Like so many Sherman Brothers songs, "There's a Great Big Beautiful Tomorrow" was an upbeat, positive, and jolly look at what the future has to hold. It was used as the theme song for the Carousel of Progress and it served as the transition music while the audience was "moving to the future". It is no coincidence that the song was one of Walt's favorites because it held the eternal optimism that Walt lived by each day. Whether or not the Sherman Brothers lived by the same philosophy is a matter of speculation. However, they knew what type of songs would win Walt over, and the results are evident in the vast majority of their songs.

Few people realize that the vocal track for this song always included the actual voices of the Audio-Animatronic characters. For example, the original lead vocal part was sung by Rex Allen, who was the speaking voice of the attraction's host. While it would not have been necessary, Disney re-recorded the track to use the new voices when the show was upgraded in 1998. The blend from narration to singing is seamless and the effect sometimes causes the audience to sing along, as if the narrator were cajoling them to do so.

This song so perfectly portrayed the life philosophy and attitude of Walt Disney that it was used as the background music for the now famous introductory film for EPCOT. The film was basically a pitch for Florida politicians and potential sponsors and was the last production with which Walt was involved. It is altogether fitting that his last film presentation would be accompanied by the theme of a positive tomorrow, as if he were telling the world to continue sharing in his dream.

The Tiki Tiki Tiki Room

The story of Walt Disney's Enchanted Tiki Room is well-known among Disney enthusiasts. The popular Polynesian show used ground-breaking Audio-Animatronic technology to thrill audiences as they gazed at tropical birds, totem poles, island orchids, and Tiki drummers singing to please the Hawaiian gods and goddesses.

We have learned, however, that technology can only go so far to please audiences that soon tire of technical novelties. Walt Disney knew this and helped to develop a standard for all attractions and shows that is still followed to this day. The key word has been, and always will be, "story", because without a story to capture the hearts of the audience, any show, no matter how technical, becomes old hat in only a short time.

The intent here is not to diminish the great work of those involved in the creation of this wonderful attraction. Harriet Burns painstakingly brought the birds to life with real feathers and an immense amount of research into tropical bird plumage and coloring. Voices from great actors such as Wally Boag and Thurl Ravenscroft flowed sincerely from the mouths of creatures so smoothly that the thought of syllables coming from something that is not supposed to talk was not even considered by the audience. Finally, musical numbers written by the great Sherman Brothers immersed the guests in an eye-candy Broadway spectacular that would have carried the show without any technology at all.

This was the legacy of Walt Disney and the Sherman Brothers. Story was everything and production was only the stage hand to success. The "Tiki Tiki Tiki Room" theme song was an integral part of the story and one of those great Sherman Brothers songs that had a tendency to stick to the brain long after it has been heard. Like "It's a Small World (After All)", the melody became so wedged into the psyche that it undoubtedly became the scapegoat for psychological issues, after a person would find themselves unable to forget it.

It is for this reason that the cardinal sin of "updating" the Tiki Room at Walt Disney World to include Iago and Zazu was never accepted by Disney purists. In order to add these characters, the main theme song was altered to the point that the audience would only hear a few seconds of the music. Fortunately, after a fire in 2011, Imagineers came back to their senses and restored the show in its entirety.

Under the Sea

This Academy Award and Grammy Award-winning song from the animated film *The Little Mermaid* is so well-known that there is little need here to describe it. It does find itself among the unique Disney songs in that it is in a Calypso style. However, the most fascinating aspect of this particular song is that it was influenced by the Sherman Brothers and their song "The

Beautiful Briny" which was written originally for the film *Mary Poppins*, but somehow found its way into the film *Bedknobs and Broomsticks* instead.

It is quite evident that Alan Menken and Howard Ashman needed no help from the Sherman Brothers to write award-winning songs. Instead, I believe this song may have been a small tribute to the brothers by a pair of writers who truly appreciated their talent. While this is pure speculation, it is important to note that most musicians are members of an unofficial "brotherhood" that is constantly including hidden tributes to fellow artists whom they admire.

The bouncy and jovial mood of this song makes it perfect to accompany various attractions and shows at the Disney parks. The attractions based on *The Little Mermaid* at the Disney parks in the United States, for example, take advantage of this song by making it a show-stopping production. Because various sea animals take part in the performance (often comically), the song is a favorite among children.

Musicians would be interested in knowing that the original key for this song is Bb. The "mood" set by this key is cheerful love, a clear conscience, and hope and aspiration for a better world.

Voices of Liberty

The fabulous musician and speaker Derric Johnson deserves his own place in our book on Disney music. However, because he is only partially connected to the Disney Company, it is perhaps more appropriate to include him here. Besides being a prolific composer and arranger, Derric has also authored nine books and has been the recipient of numerous awards, including the "Mousecar" (a Disney award) for outstanding creative achievement.

Years ago, Derric Johnson founded and directed a group of singers called The Regeneration. They toured the country performing concerts and providing ministries for churches and para-church organizations. They quickly developed a reputation as quality vocalists singing intricate and inspiring vocal arrangements, and that reputation kept them going for 12 years, while singing over 6,000 concerts.

It wasn't long before Johnson's talent caught the ear of Disney music producers and he was asked to become a creative consultant, specifically for Walt Disney World in Florida. The Voices of Liberty (known as the "Liberty Voices" away from Walt Disney World) are in a sense the "new birth" of Regeneration, and with the same quality vocal arrangements and singers, they have quickly become the top a cappella singing group in the country.

It is nearly impossible to visit the American Pavilion at Epcot without becoming patriotic all over again. The exhibits of historical documents and photos, along with a stirring Audio-Animatronic presentation of The American Adventure, causes one to rise to their feet and salute the Stars and Stripes. However, a somewhat hidden secret is that several times each day the Voices of Liberty perform a short, but powerful concert in the beautiful rotunda just inside the front doors. Their repertoire of American folk songs, Disney songs, and appropriate holiday tunes provides a motivational appetizer for the show yet to come.

The talent of the vocalists and the quality of the arrangements is unmatched by anything available today. Once again, Disney provides extra bonus for the buck in the form of entertainment so wonderful, so talented, and so...free! The next time there is a temptation to complain about the gate prices for a day at a Disney park, think again.

Walker, Vesey

There are many inspiring stories of determination in the annals of Disney personnel history. Many of the Disney Legends rose to the top because of their grit and their unusual ability to ride out storms and use them as a stepping stone to higher ground. (For some of those stories, check out my other book, *Disney Destinies*.)

Vesey Walker showed a determination at home that was truly heroic. He chose to fight with every ounce of strength he had and stretched a temporary, two-week assignment at Disneyland into 15 years of world-famous musicianship.

Walker was born on June 7, 1893, in Sheffield, England. He quickly became a great musician and bandmaster, but knew in his heart that the real place for marching bands was the United States. Just a year before Vesey's birth, John Philip Sousa left his leadership as conductor of the U.S. Marine Band and began to tour the world. The Sousa band performed over 15,000 concerts and quickly created a reputation for marching bands in the United States. Indeed, the U.S. had bands forming in nearly every major city and competitions were held at numerous times and numerous venues every year.

Some of the most popular outlets for band musicians in that day were the American Legion bands that were popping up everywhere. When Vesey came to the United States in 1912, he became the bandmaster (conductor) of the Milwaukee American Legion Band. Under his leadership, that band went on to win four national championships and the international band contest in Geneva, Switzerland, in 1934.

After a stint as the conductor of the Marquette University band, Vesey headed to the West Coast and became the bandmaster for the Los Angeles Elks band, a post that he held for 21 years. However, in 1955, at Walt's request, Vesey Walker put together a small band for the opening of Disneyland. His task was to provide a celebrative atmosphere for two weeks and then go back to his current job. Fifteen years later, Vesey finally decided it was time to retire.

The band was a hit and, needless to say, the Disneyland Band continues to amaze Disney guests on a daily basis. Because of the Vesey Walker legacy, the group is known for its musicianship, repertoire (hundreds of songs memorized), and variation of styles (Dixieland, pop, marches, novelty, and of course, Disney tunes). A concert or a parade by this band quickly separates Disneyland from any ordinary amusement park. These musicians were masters of their trade and it was often noted that the price of admission was worth just their music alone.

What was it, then, that proved Vesey Walker's determination? In the middle of his career with Disney, Vesey contracted a rare spinal disease that doctors feared would take his life. He was paralyzed for months and there was little hope that he would ever walk again. This setback would not defeat Vesey, though, and he swore that he would fight with every muscle he had until he was back to the band. He would not give up and, gradually, he began to regain control of all but his legs. It is said that he refused crutches because he was "afraid he would begin to rely on them too much".

One year after contracting the disease, Vesey Walker threw aside his cane and began once again to march down Main Street, U.S.A. with the most famous marching band ever. He retired in 1970 and died in 1977 after a long and productive career bringing music to the masses.

When I See an Elephant Fly

One wonders whether the mass of humanity waiting in a 90-minute line for the Dumbo ride at a Disney park ever stops to think about the movie itself. Perhaps singing some of the *Dumbo* songs would help the line to move a little bit faster? It is sad, but true, that most of those in line, parents and children alike, are probably not even interested in one of Disney's most important animated films.

In fact, *Dumbo* stands in Disney history as one of the most ironic productions ever attempted. It was the shortest of all Disney features because the purpose of the film was mostly to cover for the financial losses from *Pinocchio* and *Fantasia*. The concern for quality was far less, and the plot was considered too simple to be memorable. Perhaps most ironic, however, was that the film suffered from a crippling animator's strike at the Disney studio, and to most in Hollywood it seemed inevitable that the box office results would be disastrous.

Against this backdrop, *Dumbo* became a critically acclaimed and highly profitable film, keeping the Disney company afloat and providing an impetus for the features of the late 40s and

50s. *Dumbo* stood alongside *Snow White and the Seven Dwarfs* as the only feature films to that date that would see a profit.

The song "When I See an Elephant Fly" is the most important song of the film if only because the clever lyrics depict two crows singing about the impossibility of an elephant in flight, as if to mock Timothy Mouse and his claim that it actually happened. On the one hand, you have those who believe the impossible and know in their hearts that it happened. On the other hand, you have the doubters and cynics who stand by and discredit the others. In a very real sense, this was the life of Walt Disney. While dealing with a shocking strike that would claim the social closeness of the Disney studio forever, and at the same time handling the criticisms of those who claimed the studio would not survive, Walt stood out as a Timothy Mouse giving homage to what the studio has already accomplished and looking with high expectations toward the future of Disney productions.

It is highly proper, then, that this simple 64-minute film about an elephant who overcomes difficulties would be a boon to Walt Disney and his struggling company.

When You Wish Upon a Star

There are certainly not many songs that are deemed as "culturally, historically, or aesthetically significant" by the Library of Congress. "When You Wish Upon a Star" was indeed awarded with this label and it is no surprise to the millions of Disney fans who are quick to note that the song is a symbol for the dreams and aspirations of all who hum the tune. Most Disney films today begin with a castle scene and this familiar song played in the background. Athletes tell the world that they are going to "Disneyland" or "Walt Disney World" after a big game, with this song playing in the background. The Disney Cruise Line ship horns even play the first seven notes while leaving port.

Another of Leigh Harline's great melodies, the song was written for Disney's animated film *Pinocchio*, an expensive production and a box office disappointment. It was the first Disney song to ever win an Academy Award, and it has become a favorite in countries all over the world. The song was first sung by Cliff Edwards as the character "Jiminy Cricket", who was the conscience of Pinocchio. It has since been recorded by a multitude of great musicians.

"When You Wish Upon a Star" is not the easiest song to sing. The chord structures and the melody lines are quite different and unpredictable, making the song quite a contrast to many other great Disney songs. The range of the vocal part is not for the faint of heart either, which makes one wonder why the song is so popular.

To be sure, the song is one that reminds us of the possibility of our hopes and dreams coming true. It also has a way of letting us know that there is still some good in our world. But just like the Disney parks, the song's best characteristic is that, if only for a second, it takes us away from reality and inserts us into a musical fantasy. This theme was especially important in 1940 when the song was first recorded. The world was on the brink of war and morale was low. A song that tells us, "If your heart is in your dream, no request is too extreme" will go a long way toward lifting spirits and motivating action, both then and now.

A Whole New World

To this point not a lot has been discussed regarding the Disney love songs and ballads. It stands to reason that a large percentage of Disney songs would fall into this category, since the Disney stories are often about relationships, frequently between princes and princesses. However, the ratio of "great" Disney love ballads to those that are simply mediocre is sadly very low.

"A Whole New World" rises above nearly all other love ballads in Disney history as one of the greatest ever written. ("Can You Feel the Love Tonight?" is another of the greatest.) It won the Academy Award for Best Original Song and the Grammy Award for Song of the Year, and was even listed as number one on the Billboard Hot 100 chart for a short time.

Like many of the great Disney songs, "A Whole New World" is featured in many ways at the Disney parks around the world.

The song is certain to become a classic and we can expect it to be heard for decades to come.

Who's Afraid of the Big Bad Wolf?

When Frank Churchill wrote the little "ditty" entitled "Who's Afraid of the Big Bad Wolf?", he could not have anticipated what the song's future would entail. As we have already mentioned, the song became a theme song of sorts for all those in the country that were suffering from the Depression and needed some encouragement. The song became a hit, not only in the United States, but also in countries all over the world, where people who suffered from similar issues found the same comfort by convincing themselves that the wolf was nothing to be afraid of.

It is interesting to note that only two of the three pigs actually sang the song (Fiddler Pig and Fifer Pig) because they were the pigs who did have something to be concerned about. Even though their homes were built of straw and twigs, they insisted on singing this song of assurance. Of course, since the majority of citizens during the Depression years could not afford the symbolic "brick" home that the third pig built, they could easily relate to the two pigs that sang the song.

Without belaboring the point, let me note that the most popular of the Disney songs were always those that connected most to the people of day. Current events will always influence the popularity of a song, and Disney has a way of keeping up with current events, perhaps even to the point of anticipating what may be happening at the time of a movie's release. *Frozen* is one of the greatest examples of this theory. Would the same movie have been so popular at any other time?

Wishes

With any theme park or resort, there are certain events or attractions that cannot be missed for any reason. When it comes to Disney parks, the list is rather long, but at the top of everyone's list for the Magic Kingdom at Walt Disney World is the

Wishes Nighttime Spectacular fireworks show. There is already something truly magical about standing on Main Street, U.S.A. and looking at Cinderella Castle. The addition of fireworks not only lights up the sky with beautiful color, it also causes the older generation to reminisce about the pictures on television that would become famous: the ABC broadcast of *Walt Disney's Wonderful World of Color*, later broadcast by NBC; pictures of a castle being lit up at night with a huge fireworks display; and the entrance of Tinkerbell to top off the star with her wand.

Wishes is a 12-minute fireworks presentation that was first performed in October 2003. Since Disney parks were already known for their fireworks presentations, it was important for this new display to surpass everything that had come before. Wishes did not disappoint and nearly every night since its premiere, crowds have departed the Magic Kingdom after being thrilled by over 650 individual shells exploding in perfect synchronization to wonderful Disney music.

In addition to the Main Street location for viewing Wishes, many Disney World veterans have discovered even better locations that are much more romantic and provide a more relaxed environment in contrast to the crowds that line the street. One is the rooftop at the Contemporary Resort. Another is the Polynesian Resort beach or the Grand Floridian Resort beach. There is also a great spot at the end of the pier at the Grand Floridian. But one of the best locations for watching Wishes, if your budget allows, is 'Ohana at the Polynesian. Audio technicians have piped the music into the dining room and the large picture windows give a full view. Of course, it helps that the best food in the world is sitting on the table in front of you as well.

The Wonderful World of Color

(This title does not refer to the current Disney California Adventure night-time program called World of Color. While that $75,000,000 production is certainly deserving of some space here, priority is being given to a much more important program in the life of Disney productions and the birth of a theme park.)

For those of us who are Disney park fans, the significance of this theme song cannot be overestimated. In 1954, Walt Disney was looking for some money (a common quest for Walt Disney) and found a television network interested in broadcasting a Disney-produced television show. This was a significant move for any movie production studio, since it was not common for movie producers to get involved with television. At the time, ABC was an up-and-coming network with the need for some quality programming. Walt Disney wanted to build a theme park and required far more money than the studio had. It seemed that the partnership was a perfect fit and the true winners were the television viewers of America.

Each Wednesday night (the show was eventually moved to Friday nights and finally Sunday nights) Walt Disney would host a program that would bring specially edited versions of Disney productions into living rooms across the country. By 1961, even though most Americans did not own a color TV, the broadcast would be in full color and the graphical effects were quite impressive in color or in black and white. (Some contemporary historians believe that the program could have been solely responsible for the huge demand for color television sets in the late 50s.) By this time, the show was broadcast by NBC and was first given the name *The Wonderful World of Color*.

The theme song for this program was written by the Sherman Brothers who at the time were as busy as ever at the Disney studio. In contrast to most of the music the brothers were producing, this particular theme was a dramatic and inspiring orchestrated piece with full choral melodies. Like most quality music produced by Disney, the song still gets plenty of use today, especially as a theme song for the World of Color goodnight kiss production at Disney's California Adventure.

Yo Ho! (A Pirate's Life for Me)

It seems quite ironic that a song so popular among children would have pillaging and plundering as its theme. "We pillage, we plunder, we rifle and loot. Drink up me hearties, yo ho. We kidnap and ravage and don't give a hoot. Drink up me hearties, yo ho." These are the words that, if the attraction would have been built in this age of political correctness, would never have been written. On the other hand, the words prove that, in the proper context, even questionable lyrics can have an innocent flavor.

Whatever the case may be, the popular Pirates attraction at the Disney parks and the extremely popular feature films based on that attraction take advantage of this simple sea shanty that has everyone humming once they've heard it. The song itself is a prime example of how a melody so simple can still capture the hearts of those who hear it. First written in 1967, the song gained a lot of popularity when it was sung by the lovely Elizabeth Swann at the beginning of *Pirates of the Caribbean: The Curse of the Black Pearl*. Later in the film, Elizabeth and Jack Sparrow sing the song as a drunken duet, and Jack makes an important remark regarding the song. He told Elizabeth that he would teach the song to his crew, thus providing the back story for the crowd of Audio-Animatronic pirates who sing the song in the attractions.

You Can Fly, You Can Fly, You Can Fly

This brilliant song of *Peter Pan* fame is one of many Disney numbers that use an entire chorus along with the major character voices. The result is a moving and inspiring feel that brings extra emotion to a scene that is already charming. Peter Pan sprinkles fairy dust on the children and tells them to think happy thoughts. The result, of course, is that the children learn how to fly and follow Peter Pan to adventure.

It is interesting to note here that the composers Sammy Fain (music) and Sammy Cahn (lyrics) were never much used as musicians at the Disney studio. In fact, *Peter Pan* was the only time that Sammy Cahn was used, despite him being well-known among the Hollywood elite as an excellent lyricist. (He was nominated for 26 Academy Awards.) It may be that the two composers were simply too busy with other work or did not get along with Walt Disney.)

In any case, the majority of the music for *Peter Pan* was not particularly memorable and it seems that the composer duo may not have had the Disney "flair" that was so common with other composers. While most people could tell the story of Peter Pan and even describe the scenes in the movie, it is rare indeed to run into anyone that could list even a couple of the film's songs.

You've Got a Friend in Me

For those of us who lived through the lean years of Disney movie production, the significance and meaning of this song cannot be overstated. Like so many great Disney songs, the symbolism of its words moves well beyond the film and provides an appropriate accompaniment to the events of the day for Disney.

The roller-coaster ride between John Lasseter and the Disney Company is well documented. The result of the drama between Lasseter and Steve Jobs (owner of Pixar), Michael Eisner, and Jeffrey Ketzenberg (Disney film chairman) was a groundbreaking film completely animated by computer. "Groundbreaking" is an understatement, since the technological and cinematic effects of *Toy Story* are still being felt nearly two decades later.

The resulting partnership between Disney and Pixar became a gold mine for both companies and the beginning of a string of fabulous full-length animated films. Thus, the meaning of the words "You've got a friend in me" cannot be relegated to the film alone. Indeed, the fact that the tension between the two companies was ironed out and the creativity was allowed to flourish resulted in a win-win for companies and moviegoers worldwide.

The song itself became a theme song of sorts for the entire *Toy Story* film series. It was written and recorded by Randy Newman and was nominated for an Academy Award and Golden Globe Award, both for Best Original Song.

Zip-a-Dee-Doo-Dah

What better way is there to close a book on Disney music than to consider one of the happiest songs ever written? (What a coincidence that it starts with the letter "Z"!) "My, oh my, what a wonderful day" rings out like the chimes of a nearby steeple reminding us that the "Bluebird of Happiness" is just around the corner.

Another of the Disney songs listed in the American Film Institute's survey of top songs in American cinema, "Zip-a-Dee-Doo-Dah" is the Academy Award-winning tune from Disney's 1946 musical, *Song of the South*. The film was a technical marvel in that it combined live action and animation, but, as a result, the beautiful and sentimental music of the film is often forgotten, except for this song that has continued to lighten the hearts of those who have sung it or heard it over the decades.

Disney knows a good thing when it sees it, and so the song has been used for dozens of different shows and attractions over the years. It was part of the theme song for the *Wonderful World of Disney* television show, and it is heard in several attractions and shows at the Disney parks throughout the world.

Ray Gilbert wrote the lyrics and, like the Shermans, could be credited for adding another term to our English lexicon. The phrase "Zip-a-Dee-Doo-Dah" is similar to other terms that were used as "nonsense" words in the 1800s, but evidently this final version is original to Gilbert, who was also known as the lyricist who translated many Spanish-language Disney songs into English.

To close the chapter, it is impossible to resist reminding everyone of the happy lyrics from this song:

> Zip-A-Dee-Doo-Dah
> Zip-A-Dee-A
> My oh my, what a wonderful day
> Plenty of sunshine heading my way
> Zip-A-Dee-Doo-Dah
> Zip-A-Dee-A
> Mister bluebird on my shoulder
> It's the truth
> It's actual
> Everything is satisfactual

Zip-A-Dee-Doo-Dah
Zip-A-Dee-A
Wonderful feeling
Wonderful day

As a musician I cannot even imagine what it would be like to be at a Disney park without the constant audio reminders of where I am. When I walk down Main Street, I consider the music I hear as a cue to forget about where I've come from and focus on the world of Disney.
KM / Florida

CHAPTER NINE

A Word about Disney Sounds and Production

We have discussed several "hooks" within Disney music that cause us, as listeners, to enjoy the songs. While we have mentioned sounds now and then, it is worth a chapter here to cover them in more depth. The same hooks that apply to the music also apply to the sounds that have become so popular. At Walt Disney World, the sounds of the boat horns as they approach the piers on the Seven Seas Lagoon offer an exciting treat for those who remember their stays at the Contemporary Resort or any of the lagoon or Bay Lake resorts. The sound of the train coming into the station provides a thrill for those just exiting the monorail station and getting ready to enter the park. At all parks, the sounds in the attractions themselves, the cannon balls hitting the water in Pirates of the Caribbean, the creaky doors in The Haunted Mansion, the ethereal space music in Space Mountain, and the "Paging Mr. Morrow" line in the TTA PeopleMover all offer sweet memories to those who visit the parks multiple times. And who can forget the now famous, "Please stand clear of the doors" line from the monorail spiel?

By now, many people are aware that Imagineers have rigged up a way to disperse the aroma of chocolate chip cookies in the oven throughout Main Street, U.S.A., using a fan and some scented chemicals. This is certainly a fun way to create a hometown feel (and sell a lot of cookies!). What many do not realize, however, is that there are also some "fake" sounds throughout the Disney parks. One obvious example is the sound of screams from the "Everest Expedition" coaster at Disney's Animal Kingdom. It doesn't take very long for the avid listener to notice that the screams begin to sound alike after a while. And they are timed pretty regularly, as well.

The audio techs at the Disney parks are among the best at what they do. Starting from the design stage, audio takes a huge role in determining the overall effect of an attraction or show. Throughout the unique structures of Disney architecture are hidden speakers designed to blend directly into the background, whether it be plant or building. Rarely, if ever, is a speaker seen, unless it is part of an attraction that calls for it to be present. Inside an attraction are hundreds of speakers, many with different roles, all placed appropriately to be hidden and to represent whatever portion of the scene they connect to. A young tuba player in the "it's a small world", for example, will have his own speaker playing the tuba part just behind him and out of view. A dog in the Pirates of the Caribbean will have his own speaker assisting him with his well-timed howl. What is that you hear when you pull the rope at the well just outside of the Indiana Jones show at Disney's Hollywood Studios or when you touch the apple at the entrance to the Snow White attraction at Disneyland?

The always clever sound effects and audio techniques found in the Disney parks are all part of the hook that brings people back. For those of us who enjoy staying at the Ft. Wilderness Campground, the sounds of the boats going back and forth to the Magic Kingdom are truly priceless. They are the reminder that things are OK and that your day will be a magical one.

But the sounds of Disney go well beyond the parks. Indeed, John James ("Jimmy") MacDonald drew great acclaim for being the genius sound-effects technician that he was in the early Disney days. (MacDonald was also the voice of Mickey Mouse for over 30 years.) Some of the effects he created are still being used today.

Then there are the attraction voices. Few people are aware of the talents behind the microphones that recorded the voices heard time and time again on various attractions. Just take a look at this partial list:

- Paul Frees is the: "Ghost Host" of the Haunted Mansion and various voices in The Pirates of the Caribbean.

- Jack Wagner provided many of the background announcements and narrations to Disney attractions. He is most noted for his, "Please stand clear of the doors" monorail announcement.

- Rex Allen provided narration for dozens of Disney nature films. He was the original voice of the father in Carousel of Progress.

- Xavier Atencio wrote the "Grim, Grinning Ghosts" theme song for the Haunted Mansion, and also provided the voice of the man trying to get out of the coffin. His voice can be heard in several other attractions. as well.

- Thurl Ravenscroft voiced "Buff the Buffalo" in the Country Bear Jamboree and "Fritz" in the Enchanted Tiki Room. Most people will know his voice as that of Tony the Tiger.

- Pete Renoudet voiced "Henry" in the Country Bear Jamboree and an officer in Mission to Mars.

In addition to all of this voice talent, the Imagineers who design the ways in which we hear these voices are amazing. Consider that the daily parades have "zones" in which the speakers come to life as the parade travels down the street. Consider the built-in systems that allow people watching the fireworks from a resort to hear the sound track in sync with the fireworks. Once again, the quality that brings us great music also brings us great sounds.

The audio and video technological innovations that came from Walt Disney and his Imagineers would be so significant that they often affected the entire film or theme park industry in one way or another. Some examples:

- The Disney studio was the first to produce television programming in color when, in 1961, *Walt Disney's Wonderful World of Color* came to NBC.
- The development of Audio-Animatronics.
- *Steamboat Willie* (1928) was the first cartoon to synchronize sound and pictures.
- The development of the multiplane camera for animation with a 3D effect.
- The Disney studio was the first to use Technicolor, in the 1932 cartoon *Flowers and Trees*.
- Of course, the Disney studio was also the first to produce a full-length animated movie.
- With the animated film *Fantasia* in 1940, the Disney studio was the first to use multi-channel sound systems, stereo, and surround sound.
- With the invention of the optical printer, the Disney studio was able to combine live-action and animation in such films as *The Three Caballeros* (1945) and *Mary Poppins* (1964).

CHAPTER TEN

Final Refrain

There is one word that is used far more than any other when describing quality music: "classic". Often someone will say, "That song is a classic." Their intent for saying such a thing is to remind others that the song could only have become a classic if enough people enjoyed it to the point of "keeping it going".

There are many standards by which people judge music. Despite the fact that these standards are subjective, there are some songs that rise far above all others. Many of the "chart toppers" come and go, only to be long forgotten years later. Some of them experience short revivals when nostalgia brings them back, perhaps more for the sake of memories than for quality. But the truly great musical compositions have staying power. They remain in the hearts and minds of music lovers for generation upon generation. It is not just the writings of Bach, Beethoven, and Mozart that can be considered "classics", but also those of Foster, Gershwin, Williams, Menken, and the Shermans.

Perhaps my bias toward all things Disney places the last two composers in that list into a category they didn't earn? I would like to think otherwise. After all, a true "classic" is a song that maintains its popularity over several generations. It is a song that is always on the tip of the tongue and always able to cross cultural barriers. It is a Disney song.

Appendix

Chords and Chord Structures for the Non-Musician

This book is certainly not meant to be a tutorial on music theory. On the other hand, I use some terms and symbols that may cause a bit of confusion among non-musicians. One topic that is discussed often is that of musical harmony and chords. Here are some quick definitions for those who've never studied music.

Chords

For our purposes, any normal song has three basic elements melody, harmony, and rhythm. The harmony in a song is made up of related notes that provide a foundation upon which a melody rests. These related notes are often referred to as "chords", which are constantly changing throughout the song.

Progression

From the beginning of a song to the end, there is a specific and orderly pattern of chords that the composer uses to make the song appealing and cause the ear to "feel" comfortable with the motion of the sound. This pattern is called a "progression" and the vast majority of well-known songs have predictable and/or pleasing progressions. The most common of these progressions is the series of chords that lead up to the last note of the song, which is usually the tonic chord.

Tonic

The chords that make up a song usually have a predictable progression in that our ears expect certain changes to take place while we are listening to it. At the end of a song, for example, we all expect to hear a "final" chord that simply sounds naturally like the end. This chord is "usually" the tonic chord or the chord that the entire song has been based on. This is also the chord that represents the key in which the song is played.

Key

A song's key is the reference point or the tonic upon which a song is based. If a song is in the key of "C", for example, then the chord structure and the melody will "normally" come back to that note often, and especially as the song ends.

Dominant

The chords that make up a song's progression, as mentioned earlier, are usually predictable in that our ears expect to hear certain chords in certain places. In fact, most music theory experts believe that it is that expectation which makes music so entertaining in the first place. The most "predictable" chords are those which appear most often. The dominant chord, which is based upon the 5th note of the major scale, is a chord heard more than any other. (Again, this is not always true, just commonly true.) When our ears hear a dominant chord, we then expect to hear the music head back to the tonic chord. The second most common chord is based on the 4th note of the major scale and, because of its position, it is called the "sub-dominant" chord.

Secondary Dominant

As mentioned above, the dominant chord produces an effect in our ears that tends to make us listen for a tonic chord to follow. For example, if we are listening to a song and it ends on the note just before the last, we are frustrated because we want to hear the last note or the tonic note. A large percentage of the time, that "next-to-last" note is based on a dominant chord and the last note is based on a tonic. But what could we do to fool the ear into thinking the song changed keys, if only for a short time?

We could use the dominant of *another key* for a chord or two and then, to provide relief for the ears, we could use the regular dominant once again to get back to the key we were in originally. This little bit of trickery is called the secondary dominant.

Rhythmic Terms and Principles for the Non-Musician

One of the last concepts a young musician truly understands is that of rhythm. At times the concepts of musical rhythm do not seem intuitive, and since we tend to learn mathematics first, our tendency is to think of rhythms mathematically.

As with chords, it is necessary to mention some rhythmic terms and/or principles that may not be completely understood. Here is a short glossary to help make the mud a bit clearer.

Note Values

I've mentioned note values in this book such as "quarter note" or "dotted eighth note". In brief, each note seen on a page of music has a particular length of time in which it should last. One simple and truly unofficial rule of thumb for determining how long a note lasts is that the more ink it takes to create the note, the faster it moves! For example, a whole note, which is simply a circle that is not filled in, will last much longer than that same circle when it has been filled in. Even adding a flag to the top of the note will make it move faster as well. Adding a dot to a note, however, results in just the opposite effect. A dot next to a note causes it to last just a bit longer.

Time Signature

Despite its looks, a time signature is not a fraction. When we see such symbols as 4/4 or 6/8 we are referring to a very specific rhythmic format by which a song is guided. The top number in these symbols always represents the number of beats in each measure. (A measure is a small subdivision of music designated by the thin vertical line serving as a divider. Obviously, most songs contain many measures.) The bottom number tells us which type of note in a song gets a single beat. A "4" means that a quarter note gets one beat. An "8" means an eighth note gets one beat, and so on.

Every song has its own rhythmic "flavor" determined by these time signatures. In fact, it is quite amazing how dramatically these two simple numbers can affect a song. For our purposes, we need to settle at the fact that the time signature can determine the difference between all sorts of rhythmic styles such as a march and a ballad or a waltz and a bossa nova.

Disney Song Genres, with Examples

Ballad/Love Songs

- The Age of Not Believing (*Bedknobs and Broomsticks*)
- All for Love (*The Three Musketeers*)
- Anytime You Need a Friend (*Home on the Range*)
- Beauty and the Beast (*Beauty and the Beast*)
- Can You Feel the Love Tonight? (*The Lion King*)
- A Dream is a Wish Your Heart Makes (*Cinderella*)
- Feed the Birds (*Mary Poppins*)
- For the First Time (*Tarzan*)
- When You Wish Upon a Star (*Pinocchio*)

Broadway Production/Stage/Dance

- Another Part of Me (*Captain EO*)
- Be Our Guest (*Beauty and the Beast*)
- Cabin Fever (*Muppet Treasure Island*)
- Carrying the Banner (*Newsies*)
- Jolly Holiday (*Mary Poppins*)

Calypso/Samba/Latin Dance
- Kiss the Girl (*The Little Mermaid*)
- I'm Gone (*TaleSpin*)
- Mexico (*The Three Caballeros*)
- TaleSpin Theme (*TaleSpin*)
- That's How You Know (*Enchanted*)
- Under the Sea (*The Little Mermaid*)

Country/Western
- The Apple Dumpling Gang (*The Apple Dumpling Gang*)
- The Ballad of Davy Crockett (*The Ballad of Davy Crockett*)
- Barking at the Moon (*Bolt*)
- Behind the Clouds (*Cars*)
- Bill of Sale (*Pete's Dragon*)
- John Colter (*Westward Ho the Wagons!*)

Electronic/Disco
- Amigas Cheetahs (*The Cheetah Girls 2*)
- The Future Has Arrived (*Meet the Robinsons*)
- Main Street Electrical Parade (Disney Parks)

Folk Songs (various countries)
- A La Nanita Nana (*The Cheetah Girls 2*)
- Always (*Lilo and Stitch 2*)
- And Son (*Gepetto*)
- Ferdinand the Bull (*Ferdinand the Bull*)
- Hakuna Matata (*The Lion King*)
- The Three Caballeros (*The Three Caballeros*)

Jazz/Blues/Dixieland/Swing/Big Band

- All the Cats Join In (*Make Mine Music*)
- Appreciate the Lady (*The Fox and the Hound*)
- Bare Necessities (*The Jungle Book*)
- Cruella De Vil (*One Hundred and One Dalmatians*)
- Ev'rybody Wants to Be a Cat (*The Aristocats*)
- He's a Tramp (*Lady and the Tramp*)
- I Wanna Be Like You (*The Jungle Book*)
- That Darn Cat (*That Darn Cat*)
- A Toot and a Whistle and a Plunk and a Boom (*Toot, Whistle, Plunk and Boom*)
- When I See an Elephant Fly (*Dumbo*)

March

- Adventure Is a Wonderful Thing (*Pooh's Grand Adventure*)
- It's A Small World (*After All*)
- Anything Can Happen Day (*The Mickey Mouse Club*)
- The Best Time of Your Life (Carousel of Progress)
- Heigh-Ho (*Snow White and the Seven Dwarfs*)
- The Medfield Fight Song (*The Absent-Minded Professor*)
- The Mickey Mouse Club March (*The Mickey Mouse Club*)
- Spectromagic (Disney Pakrs)

Opera/Choral

- All in a Golden Afternoon (*Alice in Wonderland*)
- Babes in the Woods (*Hansel and Gretel*)
- Sing Sweet Nightingale (*Cinderella*)
- You Can Fly, You Can Fly, You Can Fly (*Peter Pan*)

Pop
- All for One (*High School Musical 2*)
- Let's Get Together (*The Parent Trap*)
- True to Your Heart (*Mulan*)
- What Dreams are Made Of (*The Lizzie McGuire Movie*)

Rock
- After Today (*A Goofy Movie*)
- Always Know Where You Are (*Treasure Planet*)
- American Dragon (*American Dragon: Jake Long*)
- The Best of Both Worlds (*Hannah Montana*)
- High School Musical (*High School Musial*)
- Ever Ever After (*Enchanted*)

About the Author

Karl Beaudry became a Disney fanatic when he found himself standing underneath a monorail track waiting for his parents to buy Walt Disney World ticket books in December 1971. The anticipation of experiencing the Magic Kingdom combined with the fantasy of seeing transportation and architecture unlike anything he had ever seen before was enough to spark a Disney obsession that continues to this day.

Karl spent the past several years studying the history of all things Disney. He has always been fascinated with the stories of the great people involved with the legacy of Disney productions and projects. When he isn't writing about Disney, he spends a lot of his time with church activities and planning vacations for future Disney fanatics. His hope is that he can encourage Disney park visitors to go beyond the parks and into the undiscovered country that is Disney.

About the Publisher

Theme Park Press is the largest independent publisher of Disney and Disney-related pop culture books in the world.

Established in November 2012 by Bob McLain, Theme Park Press has released best-selling print and digital books about such topics as Disney films and animation, the Disney theme parks, Disney historical and cultural studies, park touring guides, autobiographies, fiction, and more.

For our complete catalog and a list of forthcoming titles, please visit:

ThemeParkPress.com

or contact the publisher at: bob@themeparkpress.com

. . . .

Theme Park Press Newsletter

For a free, occasional email newsletter to keep you posted on new book releases, new author signings, and other events, as well as contests and exclusive excerpts and supplemental content, send email to:

theband@themeparkpress.com

or sign up at www.themeparkpress.com

. . . .

More Books from Theme Park Press

Disney Destinies

Find and Follow Your Disney Destiny

Karl Beaudry profiles two dozen Disney notables, from Walt Disney and Ward Kimball to Card Walker and George Kalogridis, and traces their paths from delivering newspapers, taking tickets, and washing dishes to the height of Disney fame and power.

ThemeParkPress.com/books/disney-destinies.htm

A Historical Tour of Walt Disney World: Volume 1

History Made Magical

The history BEHIND the history of some of Walt Disney World's iconic Magic Kingdom locations and attractions, including the Jungle Cruise, Crystal Palace, and Main Street, U.S.A. Learn where the Imagineers got THEIR ideas.

ThemeParkPress.com/books/historical-tour-disney-world.htm

More Books from Theme Park Press

Animation Anecdotes

Your Cartoons Will Never Be the Same

The history of animation in America is full of colorful characters - and that includes the animators themselves! Jim Korkis shares hundreds of funny, odd, endearing stories about the major animation studios, including Disney, Warner Brothers, MGM, Hanna-Barbera, and many more.

ThemeParkPress.com/books/
animation-anecdotes.htm

The Adventures of Young Walt Disney

Walt Before Disney

A carefully researched, historically accurate, but fast-moving and fun biography of young Walt Disney, from his formative years on the farm in Marceline through his Kansas City days, before he met a mouse named Mickey.

ThemeParkPress.com/books/
young-walt-disney.htm

More Books from Theme Park Press

Mouse in Transition

An Insider's Look at Disney Feature Animation

Steve Hulett's memoir of his decade at the Disney Studio is a one-of-a-kind chronicle of Disney's slow, painful transition from the days of Walt to the era of Eisner.

ThemeParkPress.com/books/ mouse-transition.htm

The Unauthorized Story of Walt Disney's Haunted Mansion

Welcome, Foolish Readers!

Haunted Mansion expert Jeff Baham recounts the colorful, chilling history of the Mansion and pulls back the shroud on its darkest secrets in this definitive book about Disney's most ghoulish attraction.

Foreword by Rolly Crump.

ThemeParkPress.com/books/ haunted-mansion.htm

Discover our many other popular titles at:

www.ThemeParkPress.com

Made in the USA
Lexington, KY
02 April 2015